CRY HUNGARY!

UPRISING 1956

CRY HUNGARY!

UPRISING 1956

REG
GADNEY

INTRODUCTION BY
GEORGE
MIKES

ATHENEUM
NEW YORK 1986

FOR GUY GADNEY

Copyright © 1986 Passy International Limited

Designed by Simon Bell

Maps by Richard Natkiel Associates

ISBN 0–689–11838–4

Printed in Great Britain by Butler & Tanner Ltd, Frome and London

First American Edition

Library of Congress Cataloging-in-Publication Data

Gadney, Reg, B. J.
  Cry Hungary!

  Includes index.
  1. Hungary – History – Revolution, 1956. I. Title.
  DB957.G33 1986   943.9'053
  86–47669
  ISBN 0–689–11838–4

Page 6
Budapest before the uprising.

CONTENTS

INTRODUCTION

It is a strange thought that the Hungarian Revolution, which seems to me to have happened the day before yesterday, is ancient history to the majority of the population; everybody under forty. Many of us know that it broke out in 1956 just as we know the date of the French Revolution. A few of us mix it up with the occupation of Czechoslovakia or the invasion of Afghanistan while quite a few have never heard of it at all. It was, all the same, one of the most dramatic and traumatic events of post-war history; it held the whole world spell-bound with excitement. It looked for a short while as if David's sling might once again defeat Goliath but then Goliath jumped into a tank and smashed David.

It was at 3 a.m. on the morning of October 24 that Arthur Koestler rang me up and told me that he had collected a number of bricks from a building site and instructed me to join him at Eaton Place and throw the bricks through the windows of the Hungarian Legation. 'I'll come if you want to,' I replied, 'but what is it in aid of?' 'To draw attention to events in Hungary.' 'Well,' I said, 'as television, radio, the papers and the public speak of nothing else, this seems to be hardly necessary.' There was a moment's sullen silence at the other end, then Arthur exploded: 'Damn your moderation!' and he banged the receiver down. (Next morning we learnt that thirteen bricks had been thrown through the windows of the Legation.)

A few days later I was despatched to Hungary by BBC television and we filmed there what we could. I was there during the days of the Victorious Revolution, when the Russians promised to withdraw and, indeed, began their withdrawal. Those were days of rejoicing, exhilarating and intoxicating happiness for the whole country. Then the Russians turned back, or rather fresh and unde-moralized units entered Hungary, killing hundreds of innocent citizens, turning the huge guns of their tanks on residential buildings and on crowds and causing devastation and death while proclaiming on the radio that they were coming as friends. Budapest, with its wry humour, commented: 'A good thing they're coming as friends. Imagine how they'd behave if they came as enemies.'

The story of the Hungarian Revolution has been described in many volumes. The question which I asked myself reading Reg Gadney's lucid, concise and moving summary of events was this: what does it all mean *today*? Was it worthwhile? Or was it just an outburst of anger and despair against brutal oppression which had better never occurred?

The answer is somewhat complicated. I thought the Revolution would become one of the most inspiring and glorious events of recent Hungarian history, rivalling the 1848–9 revolt against Austria. But not at all. When I visited Hungary again in 1964, I found – to my amazement and sorrow – that the Revolution meant little to a tired, disillusioned and hedonistic young generation. They were interested in pop-music, in the Beatles, in Carnaby Street fashion, in motor cars, girls (and boys) and nothing else.

After a wave of oppression following the return of the Russians, things started brightening up under Janos Kadar and that was good enough for the post-revolutionary youths of Hungary in the sixties. Perhaps their disappointment in the West was understandable. It was *during* the Revolution that Anthony Eden chose to start his disastrous adventure at Suez, thus saving the disintegrating Soviet Empire. The Russians hesitated to outrage world opinion but when Britain (and France) committed aggression they sighed with relief: if it comes to international gangsterism, they seemed to say, we can beat you with hands down. And they did.

The sixties passed and a new thoughtful, responsible and brave generation grew up in Hungary, a generation which cares for the country, for moral values, for freedom and decency. The Revolution and its heroes are remembered but the Revolution is not their main problem and central issue. Yet, when the events of 1956 are put into perspective, the youth of Hungary and inded the population of the whole world knows that it was a decisively important moment in modern history. The Soviet Empire did not fall apart, as seemed likely for a few days, but it never recovered from the shock it suffered. It was the Hungarian Revolution that caused the subsequent downfall of Khrushchev. But for the Hungarian Revolution (and Khrushchev's anti-Stalin speech a little earlier) Russia's grip on its monolithic Empire would have remained as deadly as it was under Stalin. Janos Kadar could never have afforded to turn Hungary into the reasonably liberal and well-to-do tourist resort it is today; in other words he could not have rediscovered the blessings of capitalism under another name. Kadar – even if he does not like to hear this – is a Hungarian patriot who preserves as much of the Magyar character and traditions as is possible in the circumstances. But he is also a faithful Communist: it is his inclination to decency, his respect for Hungary's Western traditions and the comparative economic well-being he created that made Communism almost popular in Hungary. All this could not have happened without the shock-waves and danger-signals administered by the Hungarian Revolution. Even Causescu, the Idi Amin of Rumania, could not pursue his so-called independent

foreign policy but for the sacrifice of his much hated neighbours. The world would be a different place if the Hungarian Revolution had not happened.

But if, on its thirtieth anniversary, it is wise to place events into a historical perspective it is also important to peserve the *moments*, the split-seconds of history without which great events tend to become statistics or simple raw material for analysts. It is these precious and unforgettable moments which are frozen and perpetuated for us by the excellent and dramatic photographs in this book; the confusion and fear in the Russian officer's eyes; the enthusiasm and determination on the face of the fourteen-year-old boy who carries a huge gun and is obviously quite happy to give his young life for a cause; the glee and joy with which Stalin's gigantic statue is being hacked to pieces; the young girl with her treasured Molotov cocktail are as much a part of history as the effects of the Revolution on East-West relations. Or look at the picture of the hanged AVO (Secret Police) man. The smile on the boy's face in the crowd is not the smile of revenge or sadism, it is the smile of happiness. Who knows what he, or his father, had suffered from the very hands of this victim of mob fury?

Centuries consist of moments. Historians are preoccupied with the reverberation of centuries; photographers preserve the great moments for us. And they have a tremendous advantage over the historians. Perspectives, assessments, historical evaluations keep changing from century to century, from generation to generation. Only the moment is eternal.

George Mikes

Freedom fighters with looted Soviet arms.

FOREWORD

We can refuse to accept or condone what has happened, we can keep our hearts and minds alive to it, we can refuse to countenance falsehood, and keep faith with innocence even after its murder.

Albert Camus, Preface, *La Vérité sur l'Affaire Nagy*, 1958

This illustrated account of the tragedy in Hungary thirty years ago is offered in the spirit of the advice Camus gave. It is based upon the accounts of eye-witnesses: Hungarians, some of whom were children at the time; Hungarians of older generations; Hungarian and Western journalists and photographers many of whom reported on the events in Budapest in danger of their lives.

Most agreed the Uprising was a tragic failure. It was an attempted revolution during which Communists murdered Communists fighting a system alien to the Hungarian spirit. It was a fight against the Soviet Union which denied Hungary its independence; it was not specifically a fight against the Russian people. It was a Hungarian conflict and not, as some have claimed in the West, a fight for the establishment of Western anti-Communist ideology. I have, therefore, turned towards Hungarian accounts for my sources. Of the Hungarians who gave me their accounts and corroborated others many still have friends and relations living in Hungary and wish their anonymity to be protected. The story that follows will perhaps show why their wish, sadly, to this day needs to be respected.

I acknowledge my debts to many previously published accounts: for the texts of contemporary broadcast transmissions and eye-witness observations to the remarkable anthology of documents, *The Hungarian Revolution*, edited by Melvin J. Lasky; the classic eye-witness account *Seven Days of Freedom* by Noel Barber who was gravely wounded during the Uprising; and the accounts by George Mikes, Tibor Meray, Miklos Molnar, and Tamas Aczel's commemoration of the tenth anniversary of the Hungarian Revolution, *Ten Years After*. I acknowledge with gratitude my debt to these authors and recommend their studies for further reading along with the following books about more specific aspects of the Uprising:

Aczel, Tamas and Meray, Tibor *The Revolt of the Mind* (Frederick A. Praeger, Inc. N.Y., 1959)

Aczel, Tamas *Ten Years After* (MacGibbon and Kee, London, 1966)

Bain, Leslie *The Reluctant Satellites* (Macmillan, N.Y., 1960)

Barber, Noel *A Handful of Ashes* (Allan Wingate, London, 1957); *Seven Days of Freedom* (Macmillan, London, 1974)

Beke, Laszlo *A Student's Diary* (Hutchinson, London, 1959)

Bone, Edith *Seven Years Solitary* (Hamish Hamilton, London, 1957)

Fry, Leslie *As Luck Would Have It* (Phillimore Co. Ltd, London, 1978)

Fryer, Peter *Hungarian Tragedy* (Denis Dobson Books Ltd, London, 1956)

Imre Nagy *On Communism* (Thames and Hudson, London, 1957)

International Confederation of Free Trade Unions *Four Days of Freedom* (ICFTU, Brussels, 1957)

Irving, David *Uprising* (Hodder & Stoughton, London, 1981)

Kegskeheti, Paul *The Unexpected Revolution* (Stanford University Press, California, 1961)

Lasky, Melvin J. (Ed.) *The Hungarian Revolution: A White Book* (Secker & Warburg, London, 1957)

Lomax, Bill *Hungary 1956* (Allison & Busby, 1976)

Meray, Tibor *Thirteen Days that Shook the Kremlin* (Frederick A. Praeger Inc., N.Y., 1959)

Mikes, George *The Hungarian Revolution* (André Deutsch Ltd, London, 1957); *A Study in Infamy: The Hungarian Secret Police* (André Deutsch, London, 1959)

Molnar, Miklos *Victoire d'une defaite* (Artheme Fayard, Paris, 1968)

Orban, George *The Nineteen Days* (Heinemann, London, 1957)

Pryce-Jones, David *The Hungarian Revolution* (Benn, London, 1969)

Scarlett, Dora *Window Onto Hungary* (Broadacre Books, Bradford, 1958)

Shawcross, William *Crime and Compromise* (Weidenfeld & Nicolson, London, 1974)

Zinner, Paul *Revolution in Hungary* (Columbia University Press, N.Y., 1962)

The title *Cry Hungary!* was first used as *Cry Hungary* by *Picture Post* for a special issue on November 17 1956.

R.G.
London 1986

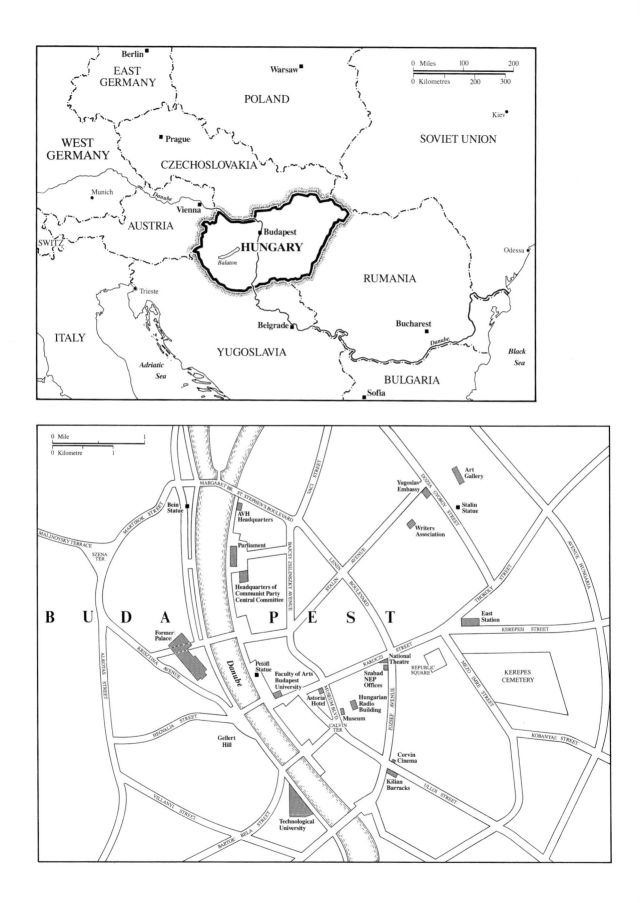

PROLOGUE

We fought by ourselves, cut off from the world.

Lajos Kossuth, Regent of Hungary. 1849

Attention! Attention!
Attention! Attention!

Now Imre Nagy, President of the Council of Ministers of the Hungarian People's Republic is going to address you!

This is Imre Nagy speaking, the President of the Council of Ministers of the Hungarian People's Republic. Today at daybreak Soviet forces started an attack against our capital obviously with the intention to overthrow the legal Hungarian democratic Government. Our troops are fighting. The Government is in its place. I notify the people of our country and the entire world of this fact.

Free Radio Kossuth. Budapest, November 4 1956 [05.19]

The Hungarian Government requests officers and soldiers of the Soviet army not to shoot. Avoid bloodshed!

Free Radio Kossuth. Budapest, November 4 1956 [07.14]

This is the Association of Hungarian Writers speaking to all writers, scientists, all writers' associations, academies, and scientific unions of the world. We turn to leaders of intellectual life in all countries. Our time is limited. You all know the facts. There is no need to expand on them. Help Hungary! Help the Hungarian writers, scientists, workers, peasants and intelligentsia. Help! Help! Help!

Free Radio Kossuth. Budapest, November 4 1956 [07.56]

The message was repeated in German and Russian. After the writers' appeal, music was played until 08.10. Then the signal was discontinued, although a silent carrier wave could still be detected until 09.45.

The Hungarian Revolution. Editor Melvin J. Lasky.

SOS! SOS! SOS!

Free Radio Kossuth. Budapest, November 4 1956 [08.24]

... everything happened at once. Russian tanks streamed into the city ... They moved to the Kilian Barracks and

the Corvin Theatre, two main freedom-fighter strongpoints, and started shelling. I grabbed my direct phone to the premier. It was about 4 a.m. I told him the city was being invaded and begged for orders to open fire ... 'No, no,' Nagy said. 'Calm down. The Russian Ambassador [Yuri Andropov] is here in my office. He is calling Moscow right now. There is some misunderstanding. You must not open fire.' I hung up, bewildered ... About a half hour later I heard him on the radio ... The nation was at war.

Major-General Bela Kiraly, *Life*. February 18 1957

To The West
You still want to come?
Too late, too late.
We are cut and fallen
Like wheat in the reaper ...

Hungarian Student, November 5 1956. *Suddeutsche Zeitung* (Munich) December 15 1956

The white terror of October and November 1956 used the white terror of the Horthyites in 1919 and 1920 as its model. Fascists, ex-chief administrative officers, police officers and army officers of the Horthy days joined with criminals against the freedom of the Hungarians and the lives of many worthy sons and daughters of the Hungarian people. And although in 1956 the followers of the bygone Horthy system felt that only the initial stage had been reached, they were unable to restrain themselves; so they attempted to 'imitate 1919' with undisguised white terror. Unfortunately they were successful for thirteen days ...

Weighing the serious nature of the crime, the aggravating and extenuating circumstances, the People's Tribunal of the Supreme Court found the defendants guilty on the basis of the trial proceedings.

The court therefore sentences Imre Nagy to death; Ferenc Donath to twelve years in prison; Miklos Gimes to death; Zoltan Tildy to six years in prison; Pal Maleter to death; Sandor Kopacsi to life imprisonment; Jozsef Szilagyi to death; Ferenc Janosi to eight years in prison; and Miklos Vasarhelyi to five years in prison.

The sentences are not subject to appeal. The death sentences have been carried out.

Information Bureau of the Council of Ministers of the Hungarian People's Republic, 'The Counter-Revolutionary Conspiracy of Imre Nagy and his Accomplices' [The White Book, Vol. V], Budapest. 1958.

At dawn on Sunday November 4 1956 the armed might of the Soviet Union struck its death blow against the twelve-days-old Hungarian Uprising. The Soviet Union assaulted Budapest with remorseless savagery. Men,

18 women and children, from all sections of Hungarian society, had fought for their freedom against the Soviet troops of occupation for thirteen days. Their dream of freedom, Hungarian and a Communist freedom, was completely destroyed. The Soviet troops terminated euphoric days of meetings, the spontaneity of demonstrations, the public and private adventures of courageous street-fighters. The dreams of these old and young men and women and the children were destroyed.

The people of the Western powers, embroiled in their own hopeless adventuring over Suez, watched the Hungarian tragedy with a sense of horror. They listened, impotent, to the appeals for help cried out from besieged clandestine radio stations and heard the signals die.

In the months and years that followed the brazen cruelty of the Soviet Union, some quarter of a million Hungarians fled their country. Countless thousands had already been denied the choice of freedom by death. Reflecting later on the death of his friend, Imre Nagy, the distinguished Hungarian writer, Tibor Meray, reflected:

'It is said that history never repeats itself. But sometimes, it seems it offers startling parallels. The Hungarian Revolution of 1956 began as a student demonstration, like that which had taken place one hundred and eight years earlier; it was followed by an armed uprising against a foreign power possessed of crushing military superiority, and it ended with the execution of its leaders. In 1849, at least, the House of Austria allowed the condemned Premier and the condemned generals of the Revolution to write their last letters; and it announced the date and manner of their execution. But the House of Moscow did not grant even so little to Imre Nagy and his comrades. Long months afterward, we are still in total ignorance about the details of their deaths. In Hungary, capital punishment is carried out by hanging, but an East German publication has reported that Nagy was shot. No one knows whether it was day or night when they died, and there was no one to report their last words. According to unofficial reports circulating in Hungary, Imre Nagy passed his last night writing.

No one, of course, knows what it was he wrote on the eve of execution. Some months before, however, leaders of the Communist Party of Rumania told Hungarian associates that Nagy, believed at that time to be in political asylum in Rumania, persisted in refusing to 'listen to reason' or 'to admit his crimes' or make 'any reasonable statement'. In answer to everything said to him, Nagy replied simply: 'Monday, work would have been resumed. Monday, everything would have been settled.' Nagy was telling them of Monday November 4, the day the Soviet troops 're-established order' in Hungary with all the

frightening military force at their disposal. By then the Revolution was all but over. Janos Kadar established a new Government.

Today, thirty years afterwards, his is, by and large, the responsibility for the present and different conditions the Hungarian people enjoy. We cannot entirely deride them. 'As a sort of reward for ghastly recent decades of terror and privation,' wrote Neal Ascherson, correctly, in the London *Observer* (January 6 1985), 'the Hungarian capital on the Danube is living through one of the most enjoyable periods in its history.' The article, an elegant celebration of tourism in Budapest, was entitled 'Taking a Sensual Soak'.

Thirty years ago, Lajos Lederer wrote a different report in the *Observer* (November 18 1956):

By evening [November 4 1956] there was scarcely a building in the main boulevards of Budapest which had not been torn open by Soviet shells. People swarmed to the Legations all day, hundreds more telephoned, imploring the Great Powers to intervene. 'Tell the world what they are doing to us!' they cried. And we could do nothing. The outside world was busy elsewhere, in Suez. We were ashamed. We could offer nothing but a promise that we would do our best to tell the world about these horrors...

OCTOBER 23

1. We demand the immediate evacuation of all Soviet troops, in conformity with the provisions of the Treaty of Peace.

2. We demand the election by secret ballot of all Party members from top to bottom, and of new officers for the lower, middle, and upper echelons of the Hungarian Workers' Party. These officers shall convoke a Party Congress as early as possible in order to elect a Central Committee.

3. A new Government must be constituted under the direction of Comrade Imre Nagy; all the criminal leaders of the Stalin-Rakosi era must be immediately relieved of their duties.

4. We demand a public enquiry into the criminal activities of Milhaly Farkhas and his accomplices. Matyas Rakosi, who is the person most responsible for all the crimes of the recent past, as well as for the ruin of our country, must be brought back to Hungary for trial before a people's tribunal.

5. We demand that general elections, by universal, secret ballot, be held throughout the country to elect a new National Assembly, with all political parties participating. We demand that the right of the workers to strike be recognized.

6. We demand revision and readjustment of Hungarian-Soviet and Hungarian-Yugoslav relations in the fields of politics, economics, and cultural affairs, on a basis of complete political and economic equality and non-interference in the internal affairs of one by the other.

7. We demand the complete reorganization of Hungary's economic life under the direction of specialists. The entire economic system, based on a system of planning, must be re-examined in the light of conditions in Hungary and in the vital interests of the Hungarian people.

8. Our foreign trade agreements and the exact total of reparations that can never be paid must be made public. We demand precise and exact information on the uranium deposits in our country, on their exploitation, and on the concessions accorded the Russians in this area. We demand that Hungary have the right to sell her uranium freely at world market prices to obtain hard currency.

University teachers and students on the march to the statue of General Jozef Bem, Polish hero of the Hungarian War of Independence, are joined by workers. United in spontaneous protest the crowds cross the Danube.

9. *We demand complete revision of the norms in effect in industry and an immediate and radical adjustment of salaries in accordance with the just requirements of workers and intellectuals. We demand that a minimum living wage be fixed for workers.*

10. *We demand that the system of distribution be organized on a new basis and that agricultural products be utilized in a rational manner. We demand equality of treatment for individual farms.*

11. *We demand reviews by independent tribunals of all political and economic trials as well as the release and rehabilitation of the innocent. We demand the immediate repatriation of prisoners of war and of civilian deportees in the Soviet Union, including prisoners sentenced outside Hungary.*

12. We demand complete recognition of freedom of opinion and expression, of freedom of the press and radio, as well as the creation of a new daily newspaper for the MEFESZ Organization [Hungarian Federation of University and College Students' Associations].

13. We demand that the statue of Stalin, symbol of Stalinist tyranny and political oppression, be removed as quickly as possible and be replaced by a monument to the memory of the martyred fighters for freedom of 1848–9.

14. We demand the replacement of emblems that are foreign to the Hungarian people by the old Hungarian arms of Kossuth. We demand for the Hungarian Army new uniforms conforming to our national traditions. We demand that the fifteenth of March be declared a national holiday and that the sixth of October be a day of national mourning on which schools will be closed.

15. The students of the Technological University of Budapest declare unanimously their solidarity with the workers and students of Warsaw and Poland in their movement towards national independence.

16. The students of the Technological University of Budapest will organize as rapidly as possible local branches of the MEFESZ, and they have decided to convoke at Budapest, on Saturday, October 27, a Youth Parliament at which all the nation's youth will be represented by their delegates.

In the morning sunshine of Tuesday, October 23 1956, the people of Budapest found their city's walls and trees had been plastered with fly-sheets during the previous night.

They read sixteen demands of students of Budapest's Technological University. Overnight the fly-sheets had been hastily typed up and printed by sympathetic secretaries in the universities and colleges. At first the students had tried to have their demands broadcast by the radio stations. But when they were denied access to the radio waves they took their demands to the streets. The morning crowds pushed and shoved to read them, as excited by the gesture of illegal bill-posting as by the insistence of the demands themselves.

The appearance of the fly-sheets was the culmination of a heady week-end. News had come from Poland: hard-line Stalinists of the Central Committee of the Polish Communist Party had requested Moscow's help to suppress the undercurrents of resentment against Soviet authority. Soviet tanks had appeared in Warsaw.

Accompanied by Anastas Mikoyan, Chairman Nikita Khrushchev arrived by plane to find the people of Warsaw, workers alongside students, organizing themselves to fight the Polish Army on the streets. Khrushchev, whose criticisms of Stalin in February had taken up most of his interminable speech at the Twentieth Party Congress in Moscow, had released the long pent-up hatred of Stalin within the Societ *bloc*. Thus, in some respects, Khrushchev had, unwittingly, inspired this new move towards a form of nationalistic socialism upon which the Poles were now insisting. Maybe Khrushchev had caught himself out; in the event he went along with the appointment of Władysław Gomułka as First Secretary of the Polish Communist Party. It was Gomułka who now steered the Party towards some new definition of socialism acceptable to Poles in the first instance and to Moscow in the second. It was a turning point: what has since been coined the 'October turning-point'. Gomułka had been released less than two years before from prison. He now became the figure-head for change. For *its* figure-head, Hungary now turned to Imre Nagy.

On the morning of October 23rd the people of Budapest read Nagy's name in the third of the revolutionaries' demands: *'A new Government must be constituted under the direction of Comrade Imre Nagy ...'* Sharing their reading of the students' demand for change, the Budapest crowds felt a surge of joy. They found a new sense of solidarity; a new and public focus for their previously silent and pent-up rage against the mismanagement of the Hungarian economy; against the brutality of the secret police forces, both military and civilian; against the continued presence of the Soviet military throughout their nation.

The students had not, of course, been alone in their expressions of anger. Writers, academics and intellectuals had met in other centres; in the open air at Gyor where Gyula Hay had led a meeting. Others in Buda repeated the demand that the Soviet troops go home. One group had gone to see Prime Minister Andras Hegedus the night before, making many of the demands the people were now reading for themselves. Hegedus told them it might indeed be possible for a Youth Parliament to be convened but he had little else to offer. Elsewhere, at other meetings, specific actions had been agreed upon. It was agreed, on the night of October 22nd, that a demonstration expressing support with Poland's new régime take place next day: it would be a march to the statue of the Polish General, Josef Bem, who fought with the Hungarian revolutionaries in the uprising of 1848. It was the first Hungarian uprising in modern history against the tyranny of rule by foreigners, a revolution that had united landed aristocracy, peasants and intellectuals.

Now the ferment of unrest united both national and social issues: the impetus for change was gathering speed as a fight to change the ruthless censorship denying freedom of expression in the media, to break up the forces of exploitation in the factories and the fields: above all, to rid Hungary of the Soviet presence throughout the country. The Soviets had arrived as occupying forces in 1944 because of Hungary's support of Hitler and the Axis. The siege of Budapest that ended in 1945 was one of great savagery. But the Germans were driven out by a Soviet army of liberation that then proceeded to rape and pillage a war-wearied population. The Soviets did not immediately establish a Communist government though various exiled Hungarian Communists arrived from Moscow including Matyas Rakosi – whose régime was a special focus for hatred, eleven years later, in 1956 – and ascetic Erno Gero who was now also to play a part in the ferment. Different political parties played a role in the governance of Hungary alongside the Communists. Of especial importance was the party supported by over half of Hungary, the peasant Smallholders Party outnumbering the Social Democratic Party and National Peasant Party. Many of the supporters of these parties would now appear on the scene of the 1956 Uprising.

The eleven years between the end of the Second World War and the 1956 Revolution witnessed the virtual complete failure of the country's economic system. It had to succour the Soviet Army of Occupation; to withstand the Soviet plundering of raw materials, especially uranium, as well as heavy machinery from the factories and industrial plants. Inflation was so bad it has been considered amongst the worst in financial history. The rebuilding of Budapest was achieved by what can only be described as slave labour. For twelve months from the summer of 1945 the inhabitants of Hungary's towns and cities faced starvation. Yet, out of these conditions, the Hungarians found the well-springs of social and intellectual renewal, tragically short-lived, crushed by Stalinist totalitarianism. The Smallholders were branded 'reactionaries'; opposition to Moscow folded under the yoke of Rakosi who felt able to boast out loud by 1952 that he had cut away his opponents 'likes slices of salami'. A Communist who had fought against the fascists underground, Laszlo Rajk, was put on trial. After a forced confession he was hanged. Other left-wing Social Democrats were purged. One of them was Janos Kadar. He too was now to play a central role in the Uprising of 1956: a fight to the death of Hungarian against Hungarian, against the Soviet Union: almost a Communist Civil War.

Three years before the demands appeared on the streets of Budapest a new phase in Hungary's political life had begun. After Stalin's death, Imre Nagy was appointed as Prime Minister replacing Rakosi who nevertheless stayed on as First Secretary of Hungary's Communist Party. Nagy assumed a softer line. He released victims of the Stalinist purges from prison, permitted the return of deportees, instituted some mild, not very consequential, land reforms. He steered an altogether 'softer' course and went further than most of the other Soviet satellite rulers. It was a short-lived interlude. When Malenkov was replaced in 1955, Nagy was removed from the premiership. He was summarily dismissed from the Party's Central Committee and was replaced by Andras Hegedus. Then Rakosi too was propelled from office by new events in Moscow: the condemnation of Stalin at the Twentieth Party Congress. Additionally, it was assumed Tito had exerted influence behind the scenes to secure Rakosi's despatch. As First Secretary Rakosi was succeeded by his friend, and, oddly, another rigid Stalinist, Erno Gero.

Thus, on October 23 1956, as the day of Hungary's third modern revolution dawned, Moscow still had its sympathizers holding on to their positions in spite of the opposition of so many different political sections of Hungarian society. Writers as well as students had organized themselves into loose confederations. Many of them, released from gaol during Nagy's first premiership, formed themselves into groups. The Petofi Club took the name of the fine poet who had played a key role in the 1848 Revolution. A month before the Uprising another writer's group, *Irodalmi Ujsag*, reformed its organizing committee at its annual congress. Along with the members of the Petofi Club it now grew more outspoken of the Government. Within days, the body of Laszlo Rajk was reinterred. The ceremony attracted a vast crowd attending as much out of sympathy for the Rajk family as in protest against the ruling order. Paradoxically it was also attended by those responsible for Rajk's death. Nonetheless it was a strong sign that an ever-increasing number of Hungarians was prepared to come out into the open with their hostility to the conditions prevailing across the country. A new generation was on the brink of rising up against the old order to destroy its legacy. But Imre Nagy by no means shared the strident urgency of their demands. The demands for independence were first of all made by the people.

Imre Nagy, on the morning of October 23, was at his country home at Badacsony on the shores of Lake Balaton in the heart of Hungary's picturesque wine-growing countryside. It was the season of the wine harvest. Nagy, amongst his friends and relatives, was guest of honour at the local wine festival. Typically, he had gone there for another reason: to absent himself from the growing political unrest in the capital. He disliked mass protest and had no sympathy with rabble-rousing. He already knew of the calls made for his return to leadership and was probably all too well aware that his influence, more than anyone else's, might be the single main factor in preserving stability. At sixty years of age he was a veteran Communist politician but, unusually amongst his kind, he entertained no particularly strong ambition to assume the leadership of State and Party. As a loyal and senior servant of the Party he was somewhat unusual in other ways. *Kulak* was the nickname he had been given: Russian

26 for the kind of prosperous-looking peasant Stalin had gone to such lengths to see wiped from Communist society. *Kulak* Nagy was a large man, over six feet tall, with a hefty stomach. He was well known for his delight in good food and wine. He had made little secret of his view that Hungary need not always necessarily follow Moscow's law to the letter. Indeed, had you stopped by at one of the many Budapest cafés he frequented you could have overheard his views on politics or football, the two great enthusiasms he shared with his compatriots. This was the avuncular figure who had even assented to his daughter marrying a Protestant minister. His face was reminiscent of a friendly walrus. What he lacked perhaps in ambition he made up for with a fine instinct for personal and political survival. He had fought with the Austro-Hungarian Army in the First World War only to be taken prisoner by the Russians for whom he ended up fighting alongside fellow Hungarian prisoners-of-war. During the 1920s he served the Communist Government of Bela Kun. Forced to flee to Moscow in 1930 he taught at Moscow's Agrarian Institute and in 1937 was appointed director of a Siberian collective. He spent the Second World War in Moscow and when he returned again in peace he played a large part in the handing over of the large estates to farm workers and peasants. His role in the restoration of Hungary's economy was no

During the first day of the uprising Imre Nagy was at a country wine festival. He was shortly to be persuaded to drive to Budapest and address the demonstrators.

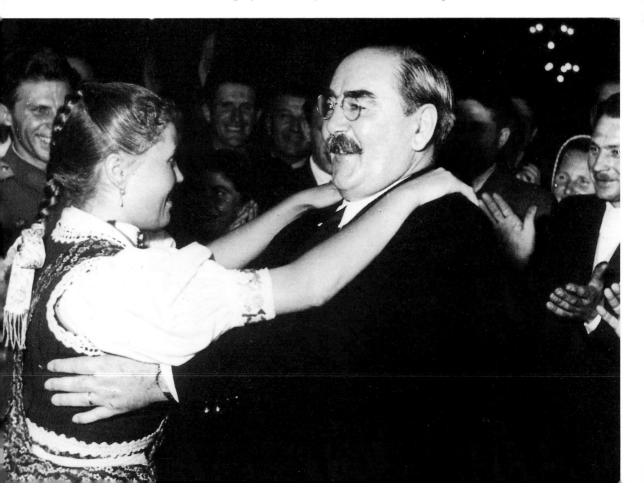

Nagy in 1954 as President of the Council of Ministers addresses Parliament. On the *left* is Matyas Rakosi who with Erno Gero, to the *right*, would both become a focus of the people's loathing.

more distinguished than anyone else's; but neither can it be said that he obviously contributed to the errors that compounded its failure in the late 1940s. Nonetheless, his association with land reform helped him to gain prestige and popularity amongst farm workers and the peasants. He was, as a Communist, if the term is today none too great a contradiction, a moderate man of caution. As such, Imre Nagy, must doubtless have learned of the students' demands with considerable concern. He was still a dedicated Communist; therefore it is likely he could not have accepted the demand for the participation of all parties in the election of a new National Assembly.

He was also a realistic politician and so could hardly have agreed, on the morning of October 23, with the demand that Soviet troops go home at once. Even though he had no enthusiasm for the Soviet presence he well understood that only Moscow could make the decision to withdraw Soviet troops. His thinking was demonstrably determined by a belief in Hungarian-Soviet collaboration and friendliness and the possibility of both. However, he did believe that he was the one Hungarian who could, given his leadership of the Party, cement the Hungarian-Soviet relationship he wished to see continued, albeit with moderation. Others, not he, were now openly demanding he assume leadership.

To put himself, physically, closer to the developments he now returned to Budapest and his Orso Street villa. There were no signs of unrest in suburban Buda. The heat of activity had, however, increased in the city's centre, on the streets of Pest. It was not long before Nagy learned, whilst enjoying lunch, that suddenly the Party machinery had been thrown into near chaos by the students' demands and the threat of imminent demonstrations on the streets. The official Party newspaper, *Szabad Nep*, had that morning described the meetings of the students and teachers as 'a rampaging river overflowing its banks, rather than an artificially channelled stream'. The paper's senior editors were in no doubt that the meetings and demands be taken seriously. As if infected by the passions of the students the editors of *Szabad Nep* also came out for reform of the Party's leadership. A delegation hurried to the Headquarters of the Central Committee. They were received by Erno Gero, First Secretary, who had just arrived back from Belgrade with Janos Kadar in buoyant mood having secured a Hungarian-Yugoslav agreement with Tito. Gero, suffering from eye-trouble and ulcers, believed the agreement had secured his own position of power both at home and in Moscow. He had not reckoned with the ferment, no news of which had apparently got through to him whilst he had been in Belgrade. Gero, flanked by Janos Kadar, Gyorgy Marosan and Jozsef Revai, listened coolly to the views of the pressmen. Their leader, Marton Horvath, advised that the views of the students and the people as a whole be treated with utmost consideration. 'The twelfth hour has sounded,' said Horvath, 'there must be immediate action.'

Gero answered the journalists by saying he thought they had 'lost their heads'. They should understand the Party and Government were entirely capable of controlling the masses. It had been decided to ban all demonstrations. When a member of the delegation asked what would happen if the students defied the ban, Revai began to shout hysterically: '*We would fire!*' he screamed.

Shortly after the delegates left Party Headquarters, just before 1 p.m., Radio Kossuth cut off some gipsy music to announce: '*In order to assure public order, the Ministry of the Interior has forbidden any public meetings or demonstrations until further notice.*' The statement was issued by the authority of Minister of the Interior, Laszlo Piros. He left the demonstrators in no doubt that troops would open fire on them if his order were disobeyed. But he was already too late.

Rank on rank, the students had begun the march to the statue of Petofi, the poet and hero of 1848, overlooking the Danube in Pest. *Arise Hungarians*, the same poem that united the Hungarians in 1848, was recited to the crowd by the young actor from the Budapest National Theatre, Imre Sinkovics:

Janos Kadar who would eventually be the chief Soviet instrument of the Revolution's betrayal and remain in power for thirty years.

The marchers converge carrying the national flag of Hungary and flowers to be placed beneath the statues of Hungarian heroes.

Magyars, rise, your country calls you!
Meet this hour, what'er befalls you!
Shall we free men be, or slaves?
Choose the lot your spirit craves!

The students' sixteen demands were read out and after wreaths had been laid at the foot of the statue the crowd, carrying banners and flags, set off on the next stage of the march to the statue of General Bem across the Danube in Buda. The announcement by Piros seemed to have the effect of bringing even greater crowds out on the streets. What had been intended as a dire warning turned out to be an advertisement for the demonstration.

Silently, from all over Budapest, young people joined in carrying Hungarian national flags, the flag of Poland or Communist plain red flags. At the Bem statue there were more statements. The President of the Writer's Association, Peter Veres, shouted out resolutions similar to those of the students. Now the crowds were encouraged by gestures of support from soldiers. They called for the withdrawal of Soviet troops. '*Ruszkis, haza! Ruszkis, haza!*' Nagy's name, too, was called out repeatedly.

Tibor Meray recalls two of Nagy's closest friends being in the crowds, Geza Losonczy and Miklos Vasarhelyi. They were questioned by demonstrators:

'Where is Imre Nagy?' they were asked.

'At his home.'

'Isn't he coming?'

'Certainly not.'

'But why not?'

'Because, if he came his presence would be used against him.'

Between four and five in the afternoon the workers left the factories and streaming homewards they joined the marchers. This was the first moment that worker joined with student. They cheered at the sight of the Soviet emblem being cut out of the official Hungarian flags; together they returned the waves of the soldiers from the barracks. No less than eight hundred officer cadets from the Petofi Military Academy joined the march. It was a moment for changing symbols. The Hungarian tricolour was placed in the arms of the Polish General's statue. The soldiers ripped the Soviet five-pointed star from their caps. Gradually it dawned on the protesting civilians that Hungarian Communist soldiers had joined in. They were not going to fire on the crowd.

Imre Nagy waited at home in his Orso Street villa, out of touch with what was happening only three miles away. More sinister guardians of the State, were, however, watching the demonstrators. From the windows of the grey Headquarters building of the AVH (*Allam-Vedelmi Hatosag* – State Security Authority) peered representatives of the hated AVO (*Allam-Vedelmi Osztaly* -

State Security Department). The AVO's trade, as George Mikes described it, was 'terror and murder'. Its operational basis was 'an efficient and reliable system of informers'. It was 'the chief *instrument* of political power', feeding on innocent victims and on guilty politicians alike, with an equally good appetite ... In 1956 it was estimated one in ten of *all* Hungarians were secret AVO informers. A citizen might only be under *suspicion* to find himself taken away, most usually at night or in the early hours of the morning, to one of innumerable jails to await the attention of torturers and executioners. The AVO, a ministry without mercy, had become a focus of passionate loathing. But the marchers heading past its Headquarters made no outward protest. Soon, in Parliament Square, many of the now 200,000 marchers would call for Imre Nagy. Only a few of them realized, perhaps, that less than a decade before the AVO they detested had been nursed into existence by none other than Imre Nagy.

It was growing dark when the marchers assembled before the Parliament Building. Its dome, a familiar landmark of Budapest, was by now a black silhouette. The marchers surged around the statues of freedom fighters from the eighteenth and nineteenth centuries: Ferenc Rakoczi II and Kossuth. They could clearly see several of the leading politicians at the windows of the Parliament Building, who now decided the lights in the square should be turned off, hoping that the resulting darkness would disperse the crowds. The lights went out. At once hundreds of Government propaganda leaflets encouraging the people to tune into Prime Minister Gero's broadcast in a few hours' time were rolled up and set alight. So, too, were folded newspapers. The impromptu illuminations were accompanied by calls of, '*We've had enough of darkness.*' In reply the lights were suddenly turned on and Ferenc Erdei, non-Communist leader of the National Peasant Party's left wing, made to address the crowds. He was summarily shouted down and booed until he retreated behind the curtains of the balcony on the first floor. There were increasing calls for Nagy. No one was going to leave the square until Nagy made an appearance. But Nagy was staying put in Orso Street.

He had to be persuaded to address the crowds by his friends Losonczy, Vasarhelyi and the writer Tamas Aczel, who found him greatly reluctant. What should he actually say to the crowds? He possessed no official rank; he was not a Central Committee member; he had only been readmitted to the Party a short time before. On whose behalf could he speak and offer solutions? What solutions?

Tibor Meray recalls that Nagy's mood on his way by car to Parliament Square was one of silent puzzlement:

'When, at last, he spoke, it was to express his astonishment at seeing a flag with a hole in its centre. "What happened to that?" he asked, puzzled; but in the moment of asking he seemed to understand. What had happened to the flag was exactly what he had foreseen a year before during moments of his darkest presentiments. The Party's opportunistic policies had driven the masses to the point of revolt and had plunged the country into a grave crisis. The October night was chill; nonetheless, perspiration poured down Nagy's forehead.'

The time had now come for Prime Minister Gero to broadcast. Another crowd had gathered outside the Radio Building in Sandor Brody Street. Budapest Radio had broadcast pro-Government accounts of the growing

By evening the size of the demonstrations in Budapest had grown. The government faced the people's united demands for sweeping reform.

By night the demonstrators carried portraits of Imre Nagy and called upon him to take the reins of leadership. The messages declare friendship with Poland and denounce *agent provocateurs* in the demonstrations.

demonstrations throughout the day but had made no direct mention of the students' demands which, of course, had already been read by many thousands of Budapest's residents. The Government and AVH correctly predicted that sooner or later the Radio Building would become a focus of resentment. At 8 p.m., the time scheduled for Gero's broadcast, several hundred armed AVO men were in defensive positions inside and outside the Radio Building. And Hungarian Army support units were on stand-by in neighbouring streets. Gero's speech did nothing to calm or diffuse the atmosphere. At the best of times his voice sounded harsh and arrogant. His cringing respect for the Soviet Union came over loud and clear:

Dear Comrades, Beloved Friends, Working People of Hungary!
The enemies of the people ... are trying to loosen the ties between our party and the glorious Communist Party of the Soviet Union, the party of Lenin, the party of the 20th Congress.
They slander the Soviet Union.

The jargon was familiar to the crowds who heard the broadcast from radios at full volume on window sills:

We are not nationalists. We are waging a constant fight against chauvinism, anti-Semitism and all other reactionary, anti-social and inhuman trends and views. Therefore, we condemn those who try to spread the poison of chauvinism among our youth, and who use the democratic freedom which our state has assured the working people for nationalistic demonstrations.

He made inevitable appeals for Party unity:

This unity, the unity of the Party, working-class and working people, must be guarded as the apple of our eye. Let our Party organizations oppose with discipline and complete unity any attempt to create disorder, nationalistic well-poisoning and provocation.

In Parliament Square the crowds looked up at the first-floor balcony and saw Imre Nagy. When they saw him they erupted into cheering. No one, least of all Nagy himself, could have predicted the crowd's reaction to what he had to tell them.

'Comrades ...' Nagy called out.

He was at once interrupted by the crowd: 'We aren't "Comrades"!' The contradiction was yelled out by Communists to a Communist.

Nagy peered down baffled. The crowd was whistling at him. Perhaps they sensed his bafflement. Someone yelled out: 'We don't whistle at you but at your words!'

No record was made of what Nagy then said. Over six months later, in May 1957, the newspaper supporting the Government, *Elet es Irodalom*, claimed Nagy saluted the crowd: '... you young Hungarians who, by your enthusiasm, would help to remove the obstacles that stand in the way of democratic socialism ...' Others said he promised reforms which he, of all people, knew perfectly well at that time he was in no position to offer. He is said to have asked the demonstrators to go home quietly. This is likely for when he eventually finished speaking after about two minutes there was an awkward silence. So Nagy invited the crowd to join him in the singing of the National Anthem. It had been a performance which satisfied nobody at all and it was followed immediately by the news that the violence had started at the Radio Station.

The directors of the Budapest Radio Station were adamant. They would on no account broadcast the demands of the students. So the crowds outside raised the chant: 'A microphone in the street. A microphone in the street!' A number of students argued with the guards that the Radio Station belonged to the people. And they were the people, the guards were the people: there was no reason for anyone to prohibit the broadcast of the demands. A shouting match developed between a number of the demonstrators and the dour woman President of the Radio Station, Valeria Benke. Benke yelled: 'What do you mean by *"The radio must belong to the people!"*?' To which the crowd replied she should give them a microphone in the street. Benke was having none of it. A member of the Petofi Circle, Peter Erdos, broke in with an attempt at conciliation: 'The radio has been fighting for democracy for a long time,' he reasoned. 'Do you think that cause will be served by putting a microphone in the street?' He told the crowd they couldn't guarantee who would broadcast what. His intervention was of little help in calming the atmosphere. Someone told Erdos he had listened to enough 'demagogy' and 'empty debate'. The remark stung Erdos.

'How dare you speak to me of demagogy?' he shouted. 'I heard enough of that accusation in the prisons of the AVH.'

This reply, later quoted in a Government publication, *Nepszabadsag*, in January 1957, reveals the extent to which the mood of the crowd had dared to swing so hard against the existing régime. As Tibor Meray recalled, Erdos' own position was hardly that of a Rakosi lackey: 'Peter Erdos spent three years in prison after the trials of Rajk and Kadar. After he was freed, he criticized Rakosi so violently that he was the only one among those who had been rehabilitated to be returned to prison. In February 1956, he was arrested and sentenced to eight months in prison for incitement against the régime. He was not released again until after the fall of Rakosi.' Erdos, facing such hostility, must have wondered, if only briefly, how far the crowd might go in demonstrating against the very same authorities that had so recently held him prisoner. He did not have long to wait for the demonstrators had already decided to force their way into the building.

A van reversed against the building's wooden entrance gates like a battering ram whilst a group who had taken bricks from a building site nearby began to hurl them through the windows. The heavily armed AVO men positioned on the Radio Building's parapet unleashed tear-gas. Soldiers in front of the building trained fire-hoses on the crowds and succeeded in driving them across the street. Then the first shots were fired.

Eye-witness accounts give differing times for the precise moment the shooting began, which turned the dem-

onstration into an uprising. The chilling five-volume, official account, *The White Book*, published by the Information Office of the Council of Ministers of the Hungarian People's Republic gives 9 p.m. in one place, 7.30 p.m. in another and 'towards half-past ten in the evening' elsewhere. Two other accounts from the Government side give times as late as 11.30 p.m. and even 1 a.m. next day. Noel Barber, the veteran British journalist wounded during the Revolution, gave 8.30 p.m. Dora Scarlett, a British resident of Budapest for three and a half years who held an appointment in the British Section of Radio Budapest, had heard Nagy address the crowds in Parliament Square. She recalled trying to telephone her office at the Radio Building but the line was dead. 'I decided to go to the Radio, and as I set off I heard shots – a brief sharp volley.' She writes she was listening to Nagy at 9 p.m. *The United Nations Report of the Special Committee on the Problem of Hungary* put the time at 'Shortly after 9 p.m. ... then tear-gas bombs were thrown from the upper windows of the Radio Building and one or two minutes later, AVO men opened fire on the crowd, killing a number of people and wounding others.'

Two tanks arrived to reinforce the army detachments. Using these as cover more demonstrators arrived in front of the Radio Building. Many carried arms gleaned from different sources, possibly from sympathetic soldiers or police or both. Later workers from Csepel's factories arrived in trucks with guns and ammunition. Soldiers and other police arrived and showed little inclination to join the battle on the side of the AVO.

Violence of a different kind had broken out elsewhere. One of the most spectacular of these early events occurred in the City Park in Dozsa Gyorgy Street. Here stood the city's massive bronze statue of Stalin on great blocks of pink marble. Fifty to sixty feet high and built to last, Stalin's statue resisted the efforts of the demonstrators who had fixed ropes around the neck and were trying to pull off the head. Eventually metal-cutting equipment arrived and there was a second attempt to fell Stalin, this time by cutting away at the bronze below the knees and pulling the hawsers attached to trucks. This proved successful. The statue fell down and was cut up into fragments light enough for the crowds to claim as mementoes. All that remained of Stalin's ugly figure was a pair of six-feet high bronze boots and the inscription:

A Nagy Sztaliniak a halas Magyar Nep
[To the great Stalin from the grateful Hungarian people.]

It had been the work of one Kistaludi-Strobl, an artist who finally achieved passing notice that evening once his work had been destroyed to the accompaniment of enthusiastic cheering.

Another crowd broke into the Congress and Trades Union building and toppled the Red Star from the front

The destruction of the Stalin Statue on Dozsa Gyorgy Street. The bronze effigy stood some sixty feet high on plinths of pink marble. The demonstrators felled it during the night. Next day, broken up, it was dragged through the streets. Bits were hacked off and became prized souvenirs. Only Stalin's boots resisted the demonstrators attentions. Eventually they stuck a Hungarian flag into what remained of them on the plinth.

of the building. Its fall was watched impassively by a group of police.

Fighting continued at the Radio Building. In the square the cobblestones were still soaked from the jets of the fire-hoses but the corpses of the fallen had been taken away. The freedom fighters, no longer simply a crowd, managed to break into the Radio Building. Some of the staff, including Valeria Benke, made their escapes from the rear of the building. Others hid in the women's lavatories.

The freedom fighters were convinced there were AVO men still hiding in the building and when they reached the locked lavatories they opened fire with a machine gun at the main door. Four women were injured. AVO men were indeed hiding there trying as fast as they could to change into the clothes of civilian radio workers. They were caught and shot. Almost certainly these were the first of the killings of the AVO men; many more would take place in the following days.

Furious raids began on other official and military buildings. The Soroksari Street arms depot was broken into; so, too, were police stations and an arms warehouse known under its cover name as the United Lamp Factory. Shops selling Russian literature were broken open, their book stocks burned on the streets. Cars were set ablaze and exploded. Fire burned late into the night.

The Headquarters of the Central Committee of the Hungarian Communist Party in Academy Street was in confusion. It was powerfully defended outside. Inside the Stalinist members made their views clear in the form of predictable demands. The 'fascist counter-revolutionary action' must be crushed immediately. Others, less militant, blamed Gero, pointing out the ineptitude of the speech he had broadcast just a few hours before. There was no disagreement on the issue of restoring law and order. The solution was a declaration of martial law. There remains some doubt as to who first suggested calling upon help from Moscow. Certainly an invitation to Moscow to give help was debated. In so far as no invitation was then issued it seems likely the idea was temporarily shelved.

Imre Nagy called in earlier to see Gero to find him trying to place all the blame on Nagy's shoulders. Nagy was now called to face the Central Committee. It had once, just two years before, supported him in opposition to Rakosi and Gero. Less than a year later it had changed its mind and denounced him. The men Nagy faced were skilled both in political self-protection and political destruction.

It was well after midnight when Imre Nagy learned that the Central Committee had formulated its recommendation to the Presidential Council of the People's Republic to appoint him Prime Minister. The meeting continued until after sunrise.

Wholesale destruction of all the signs of the Soviet presence began in a spirit of euphoria. A Fire Brigade Unit raised its ladder high up the side of the Ministry of the Interior to hack off the Soviet star. Streets were re-named, some to mark the Revolution with key dates, such as October 25 and the Soviet star was cut out of the Hungarian flags.

ÉLJEN N[...]
FELSZABADÍTÓJ[...]
LÁGBÉKE TÁNTO[...]
HATATLAN ŐRE A
SZOVJET HADSER[...]

An important announcement follows:

The Central Committee of the Hungarian Workers' Party at its meeting on October 24 1956 has elected the following members: Comrades Ferenc Donath, Geza Losonczy, Gyorgy Lukacs, Ferenc Munnich, and Imre Nagy.

Members of the newly elected Politburo: Comrades Antal Apro, Sandor Gaspar, Erno Gero, Andras Hegedus, Janos Kadar, Gyula Kallai, Karoly Kiss, Jozsef Kobol, Gyorgy Marosan, Imre Nagy and Zoltan Szanto.

Alternate members of the Politburo: Comrades Geza Losonczy and Sandor Ronai.

The Central Committee has confirmed Comrade Erno Gero as First Secretary.

Secretaries of the Central Committee: Comrades Ferenc Donath, Janos Kadar and Gyula Kallai.

The Central Committee recommends that the Presidential Council of the People's Republic elect Comrade Imre Nagy as Chairman of the Council of Ministers and Comrade Andras Hegedus as First Deputy Chairman.

The Central Committee has instructed the Politburo to draft without delay its recommendations for the solution of the tasks confronting the Party and the nation.

Attention, attention! We repeat the announcement: Imre Nagy became the new Prime Minister and Andras Hegedus his first deputy.

Radio Kossuth. Budapest, October 24 1956 [08.13]

Fighting continued, an Austrian eye-witness reported, 'along the Korut and Voeros Boulevards, and most of the side-streets were blocked by tanks. Early in the morning a large number of jet fighters flew over and repeatedly opened up at groups of civilians who were demonstrating. I couldn't see whether the fighters were Russian or Hungarian.' Throughout the morning a stream of broadcast communiqués announced the declaration of martial law and at the Government's request Soviet units were 'to take part in the re-establishment of order'.

The news of immediate Soviet involvement, and the bloodshed on the streets combined with the announcement of Nagy's appointment to the premiership served only to increase bitterness. Nagy's appointment, good news on its own, sounded a small concession. Hegedus had only been moved down one notch and the by now thoroughly despised Erno Gero was at the helm of the Party as its First Secretary. The change-round of other senior Government members seemed hardly relevant at this stage. Nagy's own view of the shift in power was probably different. Now he had at least three trusted colleagues and friends by his side: Szanto, Losonczy and Lukacs. Three others were not Stalinists: Kadar, Kallai, Donath. At least five enemies had gone. Yet seen against the events of the previous day and night such rearrangements meant little to the people. The changes had gone nowhere near far enough. His first move as Premier, the delcaration of martial law, meant those convicted of 'counter-revolution' would face execution. This first action seemed shockingly similar to any that his loathed predecessors might have instigated. When the people heard that the Soviets had 'at *the request of the Government*' been brought in to supervise 'the re-establishment of order' they naturally assumed the old order had been maintained. That they did not at once condemn what seemed to be a betrayal on Nagy's part reveals something of the extent of his widespread popularity. The placards shouted 'DEATH TO GERO!', 'RUSSIANS OUT!' The question of Nagy's involvement in these decisions and their announcement is still a subject for contention. At the time it was imagined in Budapest that he was being coerced by the AVO. A week later, Nagy himself told an Austrian journalist that the request to the Soviets had been made before his appointment. At his trial he never admitted to having made it. It was true the martial law decree was not signed by him. At the time he seemed implicated.

One may speculate vainly about what Nagy then considered to be the Soviet attitude. Clearly, it was not in Moscow's interest to make war against the rebels so soon after the events in Warsaw. Most probably, Moscow ordered the arrival of tanks as a move to scare the rebels into submission, if only temporarily, so the Hungarian Government would have time to organize itself and control developments. The tank divisions were in any case not especially well-suited to street by street combat. It can hardly have escaped the attention of the military commanders that tanks are vulnerable to attack by determined urban guerilla fighters. This, indeed, proved to be the case. In addition, the Soviets, like the Hungarian Government and Nagy, knew relatively little about the resources of the rebels whose uprising had been spontaneous, leaderless and without co-ordinated plans. What, at this stage, apparently determined the pattern of violent unrest was the weaknesses of the main centres of power; the Soviets did not wish to move too fast, too far, too soon; the Hungarian Government wanted to maintain order without inciting further bloodshed; the rebels, as disorganized as they were impassioned, wanted change and yet were without the organization to secure change. Miklos Molnar defined their position: 'The rebels, like so many of their predecessors, had neither plans, leaders, nor fixed objectives. They fought in darkness in both the literal and figurative sense ...' reacting 'according to mood. But, like the other actors in the drama they were groping in the dark.'

Was Nagy in agreement with the Central Committee's decision to call upon the Soviets? Janos Kadar, after the event, maintained that was the truth of the matter, using his view to point up Nagy's subsequent change of mind when he demanded their withdrawal. Against this, Hegedus subsequently declared he was the one responsible. At his trial, Nagy admitted signing the martial law decree at noon. Yet, it was announced over the radio three and a half hours *before* at 8.45 a.m. Again, if the account of his trial can be believed at all, Nagy never admitted calling upon the Soviet Union for help. At the time, on the second day of the Uprising it was, from the point of view of a people well used to betrayals, enough that Nagy was Premier and the Soviets had arrived. There was no doubting those facts. And it was, moreover, already clear to Government and people alike that the Hungarian Army would not open fire on Hungarians. Apart from the Soviets the only people prepared to do so would be the secret police, the AVO.

In addition to shepherding the country towards some form of order and having to deal with rebels who sup-

The slogan *Russians Out!* was daubed across walls and shop fronts. They remained until the Soviets finally re-entered Budapest and they were left with the task of removing them as the Hungarians refused to do so. Tailors' dummies were dressed as Erno Gero and labelled ERNO. They were symbolically hanged in the shop windows.
Posters of Stalin were burned in public. Portraits of Rakosi were set on fire. Soviet book-stores and official records offices were broken into. Their contents were hurled onto the streets and destroyed in vast quantities.
In official buildings the portraits of Lenin were removed.

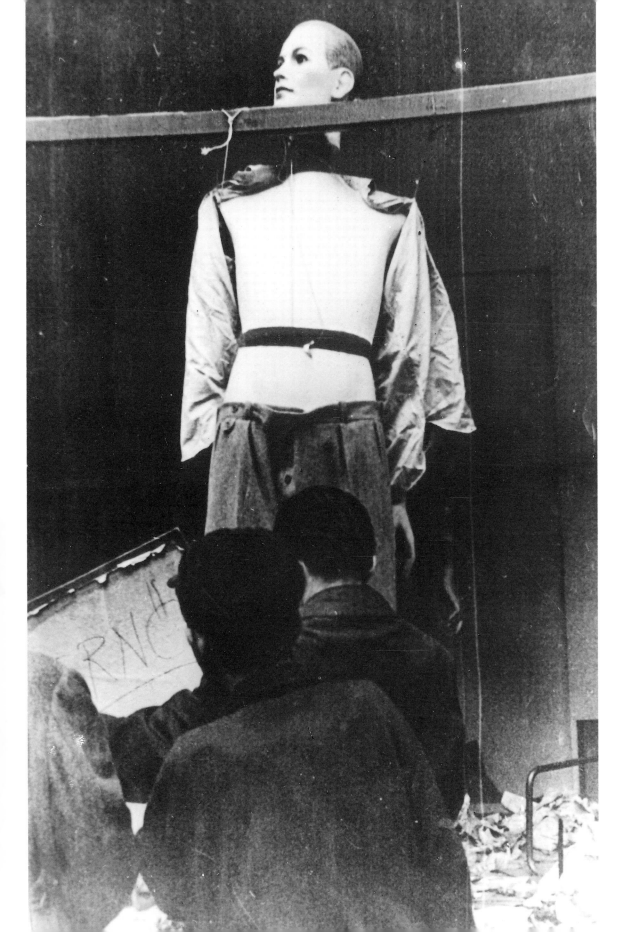

ported him, Nagy now faced news of a spreading general
strike. The workers were joining forces with the students
to form one revolutionary mass.

Soviet tanks thundered through the streets, blocking
off bridges and main road intersections. The freedom
fighters, moving in small groups, armed with petrol
bombs and guns, ran circles around them. If the tank
crews made to clamber out they were met with sniper fire
from the windows and rooftops. This game of cat and
mouse served as a major delaying tactic until such times
as an effective opposing force could be mustered. The
outcome of this city battle between Russians and Hungarians depended on the extent to which the Hungarian
Army would join in. Many officers and men were in
sympathy with the rebels; they showed their support by
handing over arms and ammunition. So far they had
not joined the battle. But the appearance of the Soviets,
foreigners fighting compatriots, friends and relations, left
them in no doubt with whom to side. It had been the
Soviets, no less, who had diligently trained the Hungarians to fight invaders on their streets. The Hungarian
soldiers from the garrisons, barracks and Military Academy showed they had learned the Soviet lesson to good
effect. By noon, the Soviets had no effective allies other
than the isolated AVO. Key points: the Kilian Barracks
in the middle of the city, the Corvin Passage, telephone
exchange buildings and rail termini were the scenes of
pitched battles and the destruction of Soviet tanks and
crews. At noon also, Nagy went on the radio. His speech
contained crucial omissions: no mention on the request
for Soviet intervention, no definition of the similarities
between whatsoever might be his political plan and the
sixteen-points demand of the students; no reference at all
to the shortcomings of the régime he had replaced, albeit
only nominally. His listeners waited for a sign that he
shared their passion for change. All they heard were the
paternalisitic tones of *Kulak*:

> *People of Budapest, I announce that all those who cease*
> *fighting before 14.00 today, and lay down their arms*
> *in the interest of avoiding further bloodshed, will be*
> *exempted from martial law. At the same time I state*
> *that as soon as possible and by all means at our disposal,*
> *we shall realize, on the basis of the June 1953 Govern-*
> *ment programme which I expounded in Parliament at*
> *that time, the systematic democratization of our country*
> *in every sphere of Party, State, political and economic*
> *life. Heed our appeal! Cease fighting, and secure the*
> *restoration of calm and order in the interest of the future*
> *of our people and nation. Return to peaceful and creative*
> *work!*
>
> *Hungarians, Comrades, my friends! I speak to you in*
> *a moment filled with responsibility.*

He begged for '*calm*', for his listeners to:

resist provocation, help restore order ... Together we must prevent bloodshed and we must not let this sacred national programme be soiled by blood ... Stand behind the Party, stand behind the Government! Trust that we have learned from the mistakes of the past, and that we shall find the correct road for the prosperity of our country.

The words of exhortation were of scant interest to all those finding they could fight the Soviets, almost literally, with their bare hands, and beat them, Even if Nagy's appeal had been effective his message was soon contradicted by the broadcasts that followed. Zoltan Tildy, the former President, asked for calm. He was generally mistrusted anyway and his appeal went unheeded. More broadcasts followed: the National Council of Hungarian Women broadcast a strident attack on 'the infamous counter-revolutionaries who are capable of anything'. The spokesman for the National Council of Peace called the rebels, 'pillars of fascism and bands of murderers'. Other speakers and pundits spoke of '*provocateurs*', 'bandits' and 'thieves'. Finally, a well-known commentator on sport threatened 'if the destruction and assassinations continue the football match between Hungary and Sweden, scheduled for Sunday, will have to be cancelled'.

The chaos halted newspaper publication. The one means of immediate communication was the radio and Nagy failed to use it effectively and this was the weapon the Stalinists still continued to use. Nagy seemed to have misunderstood the power of its immediacy just as he misunderstood the Hungarians locked in armed struggle against the Soviets. A minority may have been ex-convicts and fascist thugs. The great majority were Communist students, some of whom had been his own students; Communist officers in the army; and Communist workers whose general strike was the first in Hungary for a quarter of a century. The Party continued to use the radio to launch a propagandist attack against the rebels urging the workers to fight 'the counter-revolutionary murderers'. The appeal proved fruitless.

At 2 p.m., two Soviet Deputy Premiers, Anastas I. Mikoyan and Mikhail A. Suslov, emerged from Soviet armoured vehicles and hurried through the entrance of the Central Committee's Party Headquarters. The press of delegations all seeking information at the Headquarters cannot have escaped the notice of the Soviets as they arrived; in any case they had already seen enough of the carnage and destruction in the streets on their way into Budapest from Ferihegy Airport to have formed a first-hand opinion of the gravity of what was happening. Mikoyan and Suslov were to stay in Budapest for some three days. Both men knew Nagy who now found himself locked in lengthy debate with them: Suslov, a Stalinist who had a low opinion of Tito; Mikoyan, rather less

Mikhail Andreivitch Suslov.

hard-line than his colleague. Their arrival increased the grip of the trap Nagy was in. It meant that Moscow now had two senior and powerful representatives at the Party Headquarters, the supposed heart of political power in Hungary. The Soviets delivered their most powerful criticisms against Gero. They condemned the ineptitude of his radio speech; his complete failure to follow the resolutions of the 20th Party Congress in Moscow. Gero was immediately told he was removed from office. Whether they also criticized Nagy's broadcast is unrecorded. In any event it was now Kadar, not Nagy, who was given the task of broadcasting in favour of Nagy to make it clear that the Party supported him.

Kadar spoke on the radio at 8.45 p.m. He also got things wrong speaking of 'counter-revolutionary reactionary elements', the 'complete defeat ... of those who stubbornly continue their murderous, and at the same time completely hopeless, fight against the order of our working people'. Worse still he praised the Soviet troops as 'our brothers and allies'.

Nagy's discomfort was further increased by outspoken attacks on him from another source: the high-power radio transmissions of Radio Free Europe in Munich which seized the chance to discredit Nagy as a villain of the moment – the man who had called in the Soviet troops. Radio Free Europe and the Voice of America broadcast a relentless stream of propaganda into Hungary, believing their efforts would spark not so much a nationalist revolution but a primarily anti-Communist revolution. The American broadcasting effort was ill-advised. The American journalist, Leslie Bain, in Hungary during the Uprising, listened to the broadcasts:

> Radio Free Europe and to some extent the Voice of America greatly embarrassed the Nagy revolutionary government with their broadcasts by insisting on goals which by no stretch of the imagination that government could ever have reached.

Radio Free Europe and the Voice of America sounded just what John MacCormac of the *New York Times* called them: 'merely mouthpieces' of United States foreign policy. The American radio stations completely failed to tell the truth. Bain recalls the remark of a Hungarian refugee in Vienna: 'It would be sheer ingratitude on the part of the Soviets not to decorate the directors of Radio Free Europe with the Order of Lenin.'

The Government now had to assess the attitude of the Hungarian Army. The support it offered the rebels was both material and moral; moreover senior officers such as Colonel Pal Maleter, Commanding Officer of the Kilian Barracks; Generals Kiraly and Kana, and Colonel Marton were about to join the rebels. Similarly, Colonel Kopacsi, commander of the civilian police in Budapest, was proving sympathetic to the rebel cause. The civilian

After the first attempts by authorities to combat the uprising, the demonstrators became freedom-fighters. Men, women and children banded together to fight the Soviet tanks and armour. Many of the children had been taught the basic skills of guerilla warfare by Soviet instructors. The lessons proved to have been well learned. Armed by the Hungarian military the citizens fought the Soviet tanks street by street. The young and the old collaborated in blocking Soviet tank movements using building materials, oil, grease and even soapsuds in the attempt to halt the tanks in their tracks so they could be destroyed by petrol bombs and their crews picked off by sniper fire as they tried to escape.

attitude towards the Hungarian detachments moving into Budapest was welcoming; they jumped into the trucks and on to the armoured vehicles.

The delicacy with which the Hungarian Army in the main preserved good will with the civilian population assisted the prevention of complete civil war. The army's oath was 'Through fire and water with the people' and it was, with few exceptions, not forgotten. As far as the police were concerned they initially fought against the rebels under Kopacsi's orders. Apparently, Kopacsi identified fascists amongst the rioters and misconstrued the crowd's initiatives. In the army, General Kiraly, the

Military Commander of Budapest, also found himself aligned against fascists as well as Stalinists. (Eventually he came out into the open to fight the Soviet Army.) Perhaps the most decisive of military personalities was Colonel Pal Maleter, a charismatic officer who at this stage was Duty Officer in the Defence Ministry and thus able to provide himself with effective intelligence on developments both in Budapest and in the provincial and rural districts.

Noel Barber, whose outstanding account of the Uprising, *Seven Days of Freedom*, contains vivid accounts of the war in the streets, describes the increasing participation of Budapest's children and teenagers in the assaults on the Soviet armour:

> Teenagers seemed to take an almost perverse delight in devising new weapons to combat tanks. From the overhead tram-cables they hung saucepans filled with water dangling three or four feet above the ground, which to a man inside a turret must have looked every inch a deadly anti-tank weapon. When the tank driver hesitated, insurgents from windows above hurled down petrol bombs or grenades.

Barber tells how children stole silk bales, spread them out and soaked them in oil, thus immobilizing the massive tanks to become sitting targets for the petrol bombers. Jam was spread over glass viewing panels. When the drivers turned on the wipers the result was a thick sticky smear. And if a crew member ventured out he was picked off by snipers hidden high in the surrounding buildings.

The fighting was characterized by odd moments of unreality. Barber, again, recalls one of the oddest:

> One extraordinary battle, involving one lone Hungarian against five Soviet tanks, lasted for two hours in a block of flats at Engels Square, near the British Legation. Here a Hungarian sniper was holed up and the Russians were determined to ferret him out after he shot dead a member of a tank crew. In the street below two tanks and a mounted gun kept up a steady but vain barrage to dislodge him. Three more Soviet tanks patrolled up and down the street. Each time the Russian firing stopped for a moment, the sudden silence was broken by a whine of a single rifle bullet from behind a shattered window.

To John MacCormac of the *New York Times*, who watched the battle, the final touch of unreality came when 'in the middle of it all a civilian calmly strolled across the line of fire with a briefcase under his arm'.

Other acts of defiance continued that night until a false sense of calm, a lull, spread across Budapest. The night rain soaked the flags hanging from windows; and there were black flags too, flags of mourning.

There will be no school today.

> Radio Kossuth. Budapest, October 25 1956 [04.00]

People of Budapest, Comrades! The counter-revolutionary gangs have mostly all been liquidated. However, it is possible that, attempting to escape, small groups may try to take cover in some houses. Our armed forces are continuing with the final liquidation of counter-revolutionary groups.

> Radio Kossuth. Budapest, October 25 1956 [05.00 approx]

On the orders of the Council of Ministers of the Hungarian People's Republic, the Army, the State Security authority and the armed workers' guards, assisted by Soviet troops, have liquidated an attempted counter-revolutionary coup d'etat *during the night of October 24-25. The counter-revolutionary forces have been dispersed, and only here and there are small armed groups and isolated snipers still active.*

> Radio Kossuth. Budapest, October 25 1956 [06.00]

Dear village listeners,
This morning you will not hear your regular programme, for events in Budapest have prevented our editors and co-workers from preparing their programmes. Budapest wakes up again after this dreadful day and begins anew its constructive work ... Now peace is needed, above all. Nobody should believe false reports. The radio will inform its listeners of the true situation just as it has done so far.
(signed) Colonel General Istvan Bata, Minister of Defence

> Radio Kossuth. Budapest, October 25 1956 [a.m.]

We advise the population in their own interest not to go out into the streets unless absolutely necessary. We again draw the attention of the people of Budapest to the fact that until further notice a curfew is in force between 18.00 and 06.00 hours. The front doors of houses must be locked during the hours of curfew.

> Radio Kossuth. Budapest, October 25 1956 [10.47]

The children found new playthings in the
streets such as this anti-tank gun near the
Opera House while snipers manned the key
vantage points with rifles and sub-machine
guns.

Immediately freedom-fighters seized
control of Soviet armour they painted it
with the Kossuth arms and flew the
Hungarian flag with the Soviet star
removed. Hungarian armoured troops join
the freedom-fighters with their vehicle
garlanded in autumn flowers.

Gero tried to hang on by telling Mikoyan and Suslov that his removal from office would bring further chaos to the Party. Anastas Mikoyan told him it could hardly get worse whether he stayed on or not. Gero had prepared a document for Nagy to sign: a paper outlining the circumstances of the Government's request for Soviet help. Nagy accepted his copy of Gero's paper. But he did not sign it and settled in to work with Janos Kadar.

Kadar, former inmate of Rakosi's jails, hated Rakosi with understandable passion. He had suffered torture to his genitals; beaten testicles had left him sterile. He had only been a free man for just over two years, having served some three years of a four-year prison sentence, most of which was spent in solitary confinement. He was now forty-six years old with the appearance of reliability. He was neither an intellectual nor an academic. He preferred the cinema and to this day a special saloon drives him to the cinema to sample the latest products of world cinema at screenings every Thursday afternoon. His preferred brand of Communism, so he told Bruno Tedeschi of *Il Giornale d'Italia* in 1956, was 'Hungarian National Communism' with no place in its mixture for anything remotely concerned with Rakosi. William Shawcross in his convincing portrait of Kadar quotes Kadar's views on humour:

A captured Soviet tank is triumphantly paraded through the streets.

Demonstrators on a captured Soviet tank raise the flag of Kossuth.

I am fond of healthy humour. But there is no humour in public affairs. Of course, there are humorous events in political life, but they are in a different category.

and on fashion:

I have seen wide trousers, narrow trousers, then wide trousers followed again by narrow ones. Fashions come and go; it is not a vital matter. But whatever the fashion it must be brought into harmony with health, beauty and cleanliness. We have no use for people in drainpipe trousers. But our youth will not be like that. Those who have long hair will cut it in time.

Swedish journalists portrayed Kadar in *Dagans Nyheter* (December 2 1956) as 'grey ... wearing a grey suit, over a grey pullover, above it grey' with 'small and grey' eyes 'with a look that does not flutter, which is dead. Deep down they have an eternal uneasiness about them.'

If perhaps the ineloquent Kadar had managed to broadcast something about his beliefs in Hungary he might possibly have averted the tragedy that followed in Parliament Square.

Colonel Pal Maleter whose defection to the freedom fighters' cause elevated him to the status of national hero. He was promoted general and appointed Minister of Defence in Nagy's final cabinet. His firmness and resolve contrasted with the tones of regret that often clouded the work of Nagy and his colleagues. Commanding the Kilian Barracks he inspired his men to face the Soviet tanks with great courage. He asked his men not to call him 'Sir', rather 'Comrade' or 'Friend'. The most exceptional army officer, not least on account of his great height, some six feet six inches, he never removed the decoration he had received from the Soviet Union in 1944. He was eventually deceived into meeting the senior officers of the Soviet occupying force to discuss Soviet troop withdrawal. At that meeting on November 3 Maleter was arrested by the head of the KGB, Serov. Maleter was executed on June 16 1968.

The curfew lifted before dawn and the people went on to the streets to find food and share first-hand views of what had overtaken their lives. One man changed sides that morning: Colonel Pal Maleter. Six feet six inches tall, aged thirty-six, Maleter had served with distinction as a parachutist in the Second World War. He had informed the Minster of Defence that he 'was going over to the insurgents'. He had been persuaded when he was told to take five tanks to fight the rebels in the Eight and Ninth districts. When his detachment arrived at the Kilian Barracks, Maleter spoke to a number of the rebels. One of them explained to Maleter why he supported the sixteen demands of the students. Refreshing his memory he took out a copy of the students' fly-sheet. He had kept it folded in his Communist Party card. Maleter had seen enough and assumed command of the Kilian Barracks. The rebel cause had enlisted the voluntary support of one of Hungary's finest military commanders.

The crowds wanted to hear Nagy and began to form a spontaneous march towards Parliament Square. Alert to the growing mass, several Soviet tanks also moved towards the square. Some of the marchers clambered on to the tanks. They spoke in school-learned Russian to the Soviet soldiers; they raised Hungarian flags, tying them to the tanks' radio antennae. In the square the shouts of the mass were raised against Gero. The demonstrators were unarmed; they made repeated announcements that the demonstration was to be peaceful. By way of reply an AVO officer told them to disperse. The demonstration was illegal. The demonstrators gave back, shout for shout, as good as they got; heaping derision on the AVO officer whose men were stationed high up on the roofs of the square's buildings. Their presence incited the twenty-thousand strong crowd who hurled abuse at the AVO: '*Pigs! Assassins! Down with the AVO!*' Perhaps the crowd did not realize how many AVO men were up on the roofs. Suddenly they opened fire.

Machine guns sprayed the crowd, which could not escape. Most of the Ministries' buildings bordering the square had been locked against them; presumably the AVO men were stationed as supplementary guards on duty to protect the Government and civil servants. The gun-fire was wild and random. Three Soviet soldiers died in the shooting. The crowd panicked. Men, women and children were mown down: in all between one and two hundred. The Soviets also opened fire both at the AVO and the crowd. They fired point blank. Their fire-power broke bodies apart. Within minutes the crowd had fled. Left behind was the gruesome evidence of the massacre: corpses and scattered limbs.

News of the Parliament Square massacre spread by word of mouth across the city. The radio announced the removal of Gero and the appointment of Kadar. It can hardly have seemed particularly relevant following so soon after the massacre. A few hours later Nagy and Kadar broadcast.

Kadar went on the air first with a few offers and promises of the vaguest kind. Nagy referred to reforms and mentioned 'the withdrawal of Soviet forces stationed in Hungary, on a basis of Hungarian-Soviet friendship and proletarian internationalism':

I especially warn our working people against irresponsible alarmists and rumour-mongers, whose harmful activity is one of the greatest obstacles to the restoration of peace and order.

I am filled with deep grief over every drop of blood shed by innocent working people who fell during these tragic days. Let us put an end to the tragic fighting and senseless bloodshed.

But his own credibility was under threat. He wanted, according to George Mikes, to make it very clear to the people that it had been Gero who had both called in the Soviet troops and imposed martial law. Mikoyan and Suslov were adamant and told Nagy that Soviet tanks could establish order perfectly well. Nagy must have by now been well aware this was true. But could they keep order once it had been established? It must have seemed doubtful after the massacre. Mikoyan told Nagy the Soviet troops would leave – once order had been achieved. Nagy worked on the text of his broadcast and kept in the references to Gero's responsibility. He felt he must make it clear he had not been the one who called in the Soviets. George Mikes records what then happened:

> Two Russian officers belonging to a counter-espionage unit appeared in civilian clothes and asked to see his [Nagy's] script. Having read it, they ordered Nagy to delete all references to Gero having called in the Russians. Nagy refused once again, whereupon the Russians drew revolvers and repeated their order. Nagy still refused to obey and tried to strike away the hand pointing the gun at him. A scuffle followed between the two young officers and the elderly Prime Minster. There could only be one result, and Nagy had to agree to refrain from clearing himself of the charges. While he was making the broadcast, the two Russian officers stood behind him, their hands deep in their pockets. In all Western reports of Mr Nagy's first broadcast, it was remarked that he seemed to be speaking under great stress and with deep emotion ... The speech had only one meaning for his listeners; he did not disclaim responsibility for calling the Russians in and that seemed to mean he was, in fact, responsible for it ...

Noel Barber also records that Nagy was a virtual prisoner at Party Headquarters. A delegation of workers from the Red Spark printing works obtained permission to present a printed manifesto to the Prime Minister. They were received by Nagy in a basement. 'A dozen AVOs brandishing sub-machine guns hustled him [Nagy] to a table where he sat down facing the deputation, the machine-gunners ranged behind him.'

The workers asked Nagy whether he would disband the AVO. It was, Nagy said, a part of his programme. '... you must have faith in me. I'm just as good a Hungarian as you are'.

Nagy was being advised from every quarter and it appeared to those around him that he was fast losing patience. He may have been somewhat heartened by news from the West. In the midst of campaigning in New York, Eisenhower issued a statement. Reuter's reported Eisenhower as saying, the United States 'deplores the intervention'. General Eisenhower said that under the

Aftermath of the massacre in Parliament Square (*overleaf*). Some of the dead were buried near where they fell. The bodies of others were never identified.

provisions of the peace treaty those forces 'should have been withdrawn ...' The President added: 'The heart of America goes out to the people of Hungary. The United States considers the developments in Hungary as being renewed expression of the intense desire for freedom long held by the Hungarian people.'

A crowd assembled at the British Legation with new demands. They asked the Minister, Sir Leslie Fry, to hear them out. Fry invited some fifty inside the Legation and heard their demand that Hungary be discussed at the United Nations because the Soviet Union had acted in defiance of the Warsaw Pact. Sir Anthony Eden makes scant reference to Hungary in his autobiography, mentioning the visit of the two thousand rebels as, 'a crowd assembled outside the British Legation, seeking Western sympathy. Our Minister gave them what comfort he could ... The pitiable failure of the United Nations to influence Hungarian events in the slightest degree lit up that tragedy in flaming colour.' A few days later Eden announced that the United Kingdom would refer 'the Hungarian situation to the United Nations'. Eden, caught up with Suez, criticized the United States Government which he found to be 'in no hurry to move. Their attitude provided a damaging contrast to the alacrity they were showing in arraigning the French and ourselves.' Eden also chastised Nehru, showing himself almost desperate to criticize anyone except himself, unable to admit there was hardly anything he could have done anyway. However empty Eisenhower's remark may have been, Sir Anthony Eden did not even manage a word of support for the Hungarian people. Miklos Molnar, in an attempt to disentangle the attitudes of the West compromised by Suez, turns his attention to Moscow:

> The stakes were not equal. Factors other than Suez were involved in the Soviet decision, for a simple cause-and-effect relationship between Suez and Budapest presupposes that Moscow was only waiting for a suitable moment to crush Hungary and does not take into account the seeming moment of indecision on the part of the Soviet leaders ... In the end Khrushchev made use of the cover which Eden and Mollet had granted to Ben Gurion.

The night of the Parliament Square massacre once again found the rebels ahead of the Government, appealing to the West for help which, in the end, never came; they were still fighting in the streets, asking themselves when and how the violence would end.

Nagy's circumstances had hardly improved at all. He was still trapped. He was surrounded by all kinds of conflicting political advice. Some colleagues, like Kadar, might have been able to offer a solution. If they could they did not. Nagy, that night, as Tibor Meray found, was 'a man standing alone, very much alone'.

The restoration of order is in progress

Radio Kossuth. Budapest, October 28 1956 [04.30]

On this fourth day of the revolt, it shows no sign of subsiding. Last night the firing was heavier than ever.

This correspondent counted forty-seven Soviet tanks as they passed along the Danube in the direction of Csepel Island, which contains the greatest aggregation of industry in Hungary. There was fighting last night in the hills of Buda across the river, although Buda previously had been quiet.

John MacCormac, *New York Times*, October 27 1956

During the night from Thursday to Friday the guns thunder. Machine-gun and carbine shots ring out. Underneath the windows of my hotel room 20 to 25 Soviet tanks drive past. From the south, from the direction of the large working-class quarter of Csepel, one can hear dull booms – artillery fire. It is shortly before midnight. Curfew since 6 p.m. In spite of that youths and civilians, pistols in their hands, slink along the walls.

Eugen-Geza Pogany, Deutsche Presse Agentur,
October 27 1956

'We are not cruel,' said someone who spoke English to me, 'but the women and children killed by grenades must be avenged...'

The head of the committee explained the insurgent attitude to me. 'Three times,' he said, 'the Government has acted too late. If Nagy had been appointed Prime Minister only one day sooner, nothing would have happened, or at most a few demonstrations. For while we want democracy and freedom, we also want socialism. If Nagy had not called in the Russian troops everything would have returned to normal on the first day because we had confidence in his government. If Gero had been expelled from the Communist Party twenty-four hours earlier, there would have been no need to appeal to the Russians. If Gero, when speaking on the radio, had not described us as 'terrorists' and 'fascists', if the Government had understood our claims, the revolt would have ceased immediately. Unluckily the Government took a day too long to realize that we were neither fascists nor terrorists. The Russians had begun firing. The civil war turned into a patriotic war of Hungarians against Russians. We do not want the Russians in our country. They are taking the uranium from our mines and exploiting our mineral resources. The whole army joined our ranks and even the Communists fought at our side. On the first day the democrats fought against the Stalinists. Then, after the Russians had fired, the whole army and population, whatever their party, spontaneously reacted against the foreign troops. We are not organized. We have no chief. We have no arms. The revolt broke out of itself without any preparation.'

That is what the insurgents of Magyarovar told me.

Giorgio Bontempi, *Il Paese* [Rome] October 28 1956

In the main hall of a chapel near by, hung with black curtains and with an altar at the far end, fourteen bodies lay on the floor. Behind the curtains on the left were the bodies of two women, and one man on the floor; behind the curtains on the right, the body of a young man. Two other bodies here were in coffins. One was a young woman: the other was a child of about eighteen months. 'Send out the news of this,' said the man who lifted the lid of the child's coffin to show the lightly shrouded corpse.

The Times [London] October 29 1956

A first-aid team rescues wounded freedom-fighters under fire.

I had seen where eleven years of terror and stupidity had left Hungary, and I wanted to tell the readers of the Daily Worker *the plain unvarnished truth, however painful it might be. But the readers of the* Daily Worker *were not to be told the truth ... they were reading only about 'gangs of reactionaries' who were 'beating up Communists to death in the streets' of Budapest. The paper admitted in passing that 'some reports claimed that only identified representatives of the former security police were being killed'. Next day Hungary disappeared altogether from the* Daily Worker's *front page.*

For many years I had opposed, in what I wrote and said, and in my heart, the crimes of British imperialism in the Colonies. At Magyarovar on October 27 I vowed that in future I would oppose with equal passion and energy crimes committed by those who called themselves Communists, crimes which besmirched a noble and humanitarian cause.

Peter Fryer, *Hungarian Tragedy*, 1956

The Uprising had now spread across Hungary, gaining impetus spontaneously from the news of events in Budapest, the collapse of the Party's central authority and the swift organization of revolutionary committees calling themselves *nemzeti bizottmany*, 'national councils'. The industrial centres of Miskolc and Gyor co-ordinated local revolutionary councils from outlying districts. In both centres the rebels took over the local radio stations. (The radio in Budapest was still, surprisingly perhaps, in the hands of the Government broadcasters, and even though its central studios' technical equipment was out of action the broadcasters managed to link up the broadcast system with the main transmitter in Buda. The telephone exchanges were working unimpaired and the telephone, more than any other medium, was the main channel for the distribution of news and first-hand accounts.)

Gyor's revolutionary activities found a leader in an old friend of Imre Nagy's, Attila Szigeti, director of a state farm. Unusually, Szigeti was an outsider, a self-made politician with aristocratic antecedents, who had been allowed to make his own way as a parliamentary member even after the Communists took power in 1948. Under Szigeti's influential leadership the free radio in Gyor broadcast demands for a 'parliament of revolutionary councils'. At least half a dozen newspapers representing differing political views were being prepared for publication, and from the Gyor Town Hall a loudspeaker system was blaring out Beethoven's *Third Symphony*. This atmosphere of euphoric activity was suddenly punctured after midday by news of the atrocity in the nearby town of Magyarovar, only ten miles from the Austrian frontier at Nickelsdorf.

Two distinguished British correspondents witnessed the scene: Noel Barber, the *Daily Mail*'s intrepid chief foreign correspondent, had driven alone from Vienna into Hungary during the night of October 24/25. Peter Fryer, at the time a British Communist, on the staff of the *Daily Worker*, was also in Magyarovar.

Noel Barber saw demonstrators approach the green in front of the Town Hall. The green was lined with trees. He saw that uniformed AVO men had installed themselves in trenches at the corners of the square. The AVO men were armed with machine guns. The atmosphere was entirely peaceful. The crowd was alternately singing and chanting. They wanted the Mayor to appear and receive their demands. Noel Barber was 'talking to the villagers when the air exploded with machine-gun fire'. There was

the flutter of a black cloud of frightened rooks ... screams, followed by the thud of bursting grenades'. Still at the wheel of his car he drove on to the green: 'scores of men, women and children lay dying ... A mother, holding her baby in her arms, as though to protect it, lay mercifully dead. Behind them was a

The government Radio Station after the assault during the first night of fighting.

teenage boy. An explosion had blown off one leg and ripped away most of his clothing. He was trying to wriggle to the edge of the field, dragging one stump after him. Near him a man lay shot in the stomach; he was still alive, muttering incomprehensibly. His entrails were hanging out. There seemed to be legs and arms everywhere. In all eighty-two innocent people had been murdered; another two hundred were hurt, many of them maimed for life.

The survivors immediately took revenge and hunted down the AVO men. But when they reached the barracks they found only three officers attempting to make good their escape, one of whom jumped from a third floor window. Bruno Tedeschi, *Il Giornale d'Italia*'s correspondent, saw what had happened to the AVO officer. 'His body landed on the pavement and parts of his brains had squirted out of his open skull . . . the two others were captured. The crowd threw itself upon them. They were

beaten until their bodies were mere sanguinary objects. Then they were split into pieces as if this had been the work of wild animals.' The crowd found two AVO had been taken to hospital. They removed one of them, carried him to the square, and strung him from a tree by his ankles.

Peter Fryer went with the townspeople to the Magyarovar cemetery, its chapel and mortuary. He recalls:

Hundreds went with us; we passed many more coming away, having identified kinsfolk or sweethearts or friends or having stood in homage to dead workmates or fellow-students. Some faces were red and stern, others were contorted with weeping, and I wept myself when we reached the chapel and the mortuary. The mourners made way for us and gently pushed us to the front, so that we should see and know and tell what we had seen. The bodies lay in rows; the dried blood was still on the clothing. Some had little bunches of flowers on

Magyarovar: the dead are identified while the Soviet tanks continued their assault.

John Sadovy, the *Life* magazine photographer found himself, by chance, amongst a group of freedom fighters called to the secret police, AVO, headquarters. When the secret policemen came out of the building they were shot dead at point blank range. Sadovy continued to photograph the killing of the AVO men whilst standing by the elbow of the freedom fighters. His complete photographic record of the vengeance killings are here published for the first time in the sequence he took the photos.

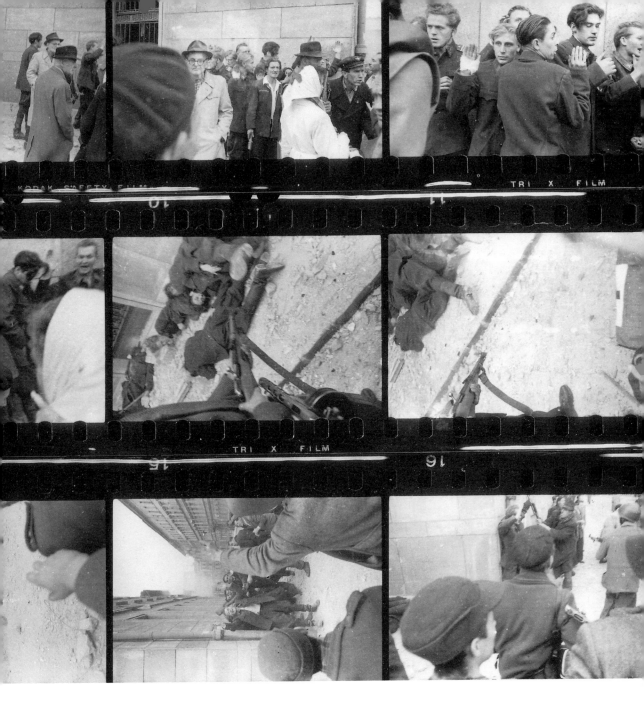

their breasts. There were boys who could not have been more than sixteen. There was a boy of six or so. Already in a coffin, lightly shrouded, lay the corpse of an eighteen-month-old baby. After eleven years of 'people's democracy' it had come to this: the security police was so remote from the people, so alien to them, so vicious and so brutal that it turned its weapons on a defenceless crowd and murdered the people who were supposed to be the masters of their own country.'

Within the hour news of what had happened in Magyarovar reached Budapest and the rebels unleashed their hatred of the AVO with extreme savagery. Innumerable secret policemen were hunted out, lynched or hanged from the branches of trees in the streets and squares. The crowds stood in silence peering at the bloodied corpses. Many spat at them. Some AVO men tried to disguise themselves hurriedly in plain clothes. One who had done so failed to change his boots. The boots were spotted. He was chased, caught and lynched. One refugee, at the time twelve years old yet still seeking anonymity, remembers:

I lived with my father, mother and elder brother in a large apartment block. It was served by a central elevator shaft and, lying in my bed I could hear the elevator machinery. After the hour of curfew the elevator machinery went silent. Everyone was supposed to be off the streets. My father believed our janitor was an AVO informer. At any rate we were always told to be careful what we said when he was within earshot. I remember the feeling of terror when the elevator machinery started up during the hours of curfew. It meant the AVO had awakened the janitor, unlocked the gates, and were coming up, through the floors, to take a neighbour away. You might hear voices. It would be the last time you would hear the neighbour speak. If they were taken away it meant you would never see them again. It was enough that the janitor might have heard, or thought he heard, someone listening to clandestine radio broadcasts; even Radio Free Europe or the Voice of America. It is hard, thirty years afterwards, to express the dread we felt for the AVO. I think I may have buried my fear in my unconscious mind. But I can still feel it, even today.

Throughout the day, the rebels opened up the prisons and freed between five and six thousand men and women. Many had been taken away in the night or at dawn and had faced no trial. Peter Fryer watched 450 men freed from Budapest's prison, Gyustofoghaz. 'Some of them were raving mad and had to be restrained and taken into gentler custody.' Several hundred men and women, forgotten by the outside world, came out of the Vac fortress, north of Budapest. Pal Ignotus remembered Vac: 'A society of frieze-dressed cripples, caricatures of the social values which had dwindled and collapsed before

AVO men were brought out of their headquarters and summarily shot. Some freedom fighters emptied their handguns into the corpses in gestures of hate. Those suspected of being amongst the many thousands of secret police informers were marched through the streets before summary execution. Long after the secret policemen had been flushed out of their headquarters it was suspected that some had sought sanctuary by barricading themselves into secret underground cells. The freedom fighters dug up the street outside to get to them. Groups of AVO were thrown to their death from buildings where they had been hiding. Secret dossiers were hurled down onto their corpses.

and during our imprisonment. We dragged ourselves along in our sweat-soaked, ill-fitting uniforms, with our bristly, emaciated faces, often trembling in the hope of an extra dixie-full of food.'

Nagy attended meetings of the Central Committee. Gero and Hegedus had left, protected by Soviet troops. He managed to gain approval for a statement in general favour of Workers' Councils, the promise of a new national Government, talks with Moscow on some redefinition of its relationship with Hungary and an extension of the amnesty to ten o'clock that night. He argued for a Government with a broader constituency, and the arguments dragged on. He hoped to be able to make an announcement of his re-formed Cabinet the following day.

Outside Hungary, in the West, the events encouraged official declarations of support for the Hungarian people: in the main they were hedged about with caution but their attacks on Soviet policy offered encouragement and some hope that positive action on their behalf might possibly be taken.

The fighting continued in the streets. Noel Barber found himself in his hired car on the Chain Bridge across

The years of pent up rage against the tyranny of Stalinist policing, the web of informers, the murders in gaols, tortures and law enforcement from Moscow exploded into horrendous violence. Secret policemen, their informers and sympathisers were dragged to trees, hanged upside down and beaten to death. Their corpses were left bleeding to be spat on and laughed at. Neither the Soviet occupying forces nor Nagy's regime could find a remedy to prevent the nightmarish rejoicing.

the Danube. He was caught in cross-fire from Soviet troops and freedom fighters. He switched off the lights of his car and crawled to the barricade:

> I found nine boys there, their average age about eighteen. Three wore Hungarian uniforms, but with the hated red star torn off. Others wore red, green and white armbands, the national colours of Hungary. All had sub-machine guns. Their pockets bulged with ammunition.
>
> Half-way across the bridge I could see the dim outlines of two Soviet tanks. For an hour they fired at us until a shell smashed straight into the oveturned bus. One of the boys was killed instantly. I tried to help a second boy who was hurt, but he died five minutes later in my arms.

The street fighting produced some unusual leaders who organized *ad hoc* groups to keep up the fight against the Soviet tanks. One character, an elderly man known simply as 'Uncle Szabo', operated in the Szena Square area. Uncle Szabo specialized in knocking out tanks. George Mikes recalls:

> Everybody in Budapest had by now learned that the big Russian tanks had a petrol-cap on one side. It was even obligingly marked 'Petrol', and made an excellent target for Molotov cocktails. The Russians, too, learned their lesson: after a day or two no tanks moved singly, but only in convoys. One tank alone is helpless under close-range attack, but in a convoy they can easily defend each other. Even so, Uncle Szabo and his few thousand undisciplined warriors, workers, office clerks, mostly young men under twenty-two, are reported to have knocked out about thirty giant Russian tanks before Saturday night. Uncle Szabo and his men could not be dispersed either by the Russians or by the AVO. It happened once or twice that they had to evacuate Szena Square, but they always returned to continue the fight.

The radio kept up what George Mikes calls 'its incredible role: it seemed to be independent of the Government and under the personal direction of Szepesi, the sports commentator who went on explaining that the revolution was very badly timed just before the Olympic Games.' Outside Budapest, as in Gyor, Miskolc and Pecs, the stations were in the control of the rebels. In Budapest the streams of abuse continued to be hurled at the 'counter-revolutionaries', some of it wholly counter-effective; some of it, especially the tirades of the absurd Szepesi, was laughable. But, by the end of the day, the opposing sides were perhaps now more clearly defined. It was Hungary and Hungarians against the Soviets and the AVO. And the foreign journalists were very successfully keeping the rest of the world informed.

Enough bloodshed! Enough ransacked streets! We would love to know whether our children, whether our relatives are still alive. We would love to be together again ... We would love to enjoy life again. We would like not to fear death any longer ... In Hungary, after order has been restored, life will be more beautiful, more human, more Hungarian than ever it was before.

Radio Kossuth. Budapest, October 27 1956 [07.00]

According to reports from various parts of the city, last night was quieter than the previous one ... Liquidation is still in progress of groups still fighting after expiration of the amnesty deadline at 22.00 hours.

Radio Kossuth. Budapest, October 27 1956 [07.29]

The inhabitants of Budapest and several provincial towns have drawn our attention to the fact that armed groups in the capital and elsewhere are distributing leaflets containing statements purporting to emanate from the Government and other organs. These are causing confusion. We have been authorized to announce they are forgeries.

Radio Kossuth. Budapest, October 27 1956 [10.00]

'We knew we were strong and the government was weak,' said Peter ... When word reached the [Kilian] barracks that Russian tanks were coming, the colonel [Pal Maleter] ordered complete quiet. The tanks came close to the barracks wall, but no one stirred. Some infantry appeared and shot up the building but the freedom fighters did not return the fire. Finally there were twenty tanks, some seventy-five infantrymen, a truck, and an armoured car outside the barracks. 'Colonel Maleter came and looked down,' recalls Peter Szanto. 'He picked up a small nitro-glycerine bottle and threw it at the truck. The truck disappeared in one big roar. Then we all threw nitro-glycerine bottles and benzine and used machine pistols on the infantry. It was a fine trick. We killed the infantry, got the truck, the armoured car, and four of the tanks in about five minutes.'

Time Magazine, January 7 1957

A Soviet gun carrier and military vehicle are set ablaze (*overleaf*) whilst civilians pass by unconcerned and a tank squadron rumbles into action down nearby streets.

Nagy and his Government seemed, painfully and inevitably, to be following the tide of the Revolution, power-

less to influence it, and always issuing accounts of their initiatives almost exactly twenty-four hours too late. What was happening on the streets was unbelievable and of immediate consequence and, understandably, Cabinet changes, though believable, seemed virtually of no consequence at all. Nagy thought they were and at noon broadcast the changes. OUT: Hegedus, Gero, Piros, Bata, Hidas, Marosan, Mekis, Szijarto, Berei, Darvas. It ought to have counted that Nagy had sacked the head of the AVH (Piros), Bata (Minister of Defence who had been responsible for ordering Hungarian soldiers to shoot down their compatriots), and the others of whom Szijarto (Minister of Construction) had been particularly disliked. IN: Kovacs, Babits, Lukacs, Ribiansky. Of those remaining there was a group still identifiable as old followers of Rakosi: Horvath, Csergo, Czottner, Apro, Bebrits. There was hardly a personal friend of Nagy's amongst them. Perhaps he thought he wanted to be seen to be scrupulously avoiding any charges of creating a personality cult. In that he succeeded. Sadly, as Tibor Meray put it, 'Nagy could still visualize only those measures which conformed to the ideals of the Party that had banished him, vilified him, and dragged him through the mud ...' He was still the prisoner of the Party and, as though the pattern of his actions was inevitable, his new Defence Minister, General Janza, issued a communiqué:

> If those armed groups which are still resisting do not lay down their arms after being summoned to do so by the Hungarian army units, they will be completely liquidated.

Colonel Maleter, leading the centre of resistance at the Kilian Barracks, spoke in fluent German to the Austrian journalist Eugen-Geza Pogany: 'For us there is only one alternative – either we win, or we fall. There is no third possibility. We have confidence in Imre Nagy, but we will lay down our weapons only to regular Hungarian troops, and we will put ourselves at the disposal of the new Government immediately if it is really a Hungarian government.'

Maleter announced his plan whilst Soviet tanks were levelling houses all around the barracks he commanded.

Nagy faced another setback when Bela Kovacs telephoned him from Pecs with the refusal of his appointment as Minister of Agriculture. This removed one appointee who had formerly been General Secretary of the Small Holders Party. News was also filtering through to the Government that the radio stations in the provinces were co-ordinating their efforts with the revolutionary councils and committees. Indeed, the Central Council of Trade Unions offered the workers' councils its support. The success of this collaboration could even be seen in the food-stores. FOR EXPORT ONLY provisions had been diverted to the people and food-stuffs, the like of which

Torn-up tram rails, burned-out trucks and over-turned trams block the streets against the Soviet advance.

had hardly been seen since before the war, were being made available.

Perhaps Nagy saw himself as an avuncular mediator. In this he was, to some extent, well-advised. He steered a middle course, neither, on the one hand, subscribing to the more extreme revolutionary aspirations of the rebels; nor, on the other hand, agreeing to the calls for the liquidation of the rebels, calls issued as threats over the Government radio by General Janza. Nagy insisted upon a cease-fire. He made it plain to a delegation of rebels who visited him during the afternoon. The Soviets would not leave unless there was cease-fire.

Perhaps he really did get it right that day. Miklos Molnar described the first balance sheet of 'this strange Government ...' It had started with 'fighting the rebels and ended with a reconciliation which adopted most of their major claims'. It was not far short, Molnar concluded, 'of the optimum solution, if we think of politics as the art of the possible'.

Nagy could easily draw his own conclusions about the success or failure of the Soviet armoured and tank forces occupying Hungary. They had failed. Their failure would encourage Moscow either to withdraw to ensure no further losses or to send in reinforcements and wipe out the rebel forces once and for all.

Perhaps, he thought, if he held on a few more days or hours, the Soviet Union would itself make up its mind. He therefore turned his attention to a swift reorganization of the Party machinery, and waited.

Soviet tanks were abandoned and used to block the streets.

The Government of the Hungarian People's Republic orders an immediate general cease-fire to stop further bloodshed and ensure peaceful development. It instructs the armed forces that they should fire if attacked.
[Signed] Imre Nagy, President of the Council of Ministers.

Radio Kossuth. Budapest, October 28 1956 [13.20]

Mr Sobolev (USSR): *What then is the true purpose of the United States, United Kingdom and French Governments in raising the question of the internal situation in Hungary in the Security Council? In our view, the purpose of their action is to give further encouragement to the armed rebellion which is being conducted by a reactionary underground movement against the legal Hungarian Government. Is such a step consistent with normal diplomatic relations between sovereign Governments? Of course not ... It is a provocative step intended in reality not to maintain international peace and security but to ferment criminal activities by elements of a fascist type in Hungary and to exacerbate the international situation ...*

Dr Brilej (Yugoslavia): *We are confident, however, that the Hungarian Government and the Hungarian people will find a solution to the present difficulties in conformity with the best interests of their country. We do not, therefore view with favour the bringing of this item, 'The situation in Hungary', before the Security Council.*

Mr Sobolev: *... the meeting has proceeded so quickly – and I blame myself for this – that I failed to draw your attention to the fact that I wanted to make a procedural proposal before the authors of the letter made their substantive statements. I wanted to propose that in accordance with rule 33 of the rules of procedure we should postpone discussion of this question for a certain period, say, three or four days, in order to enable all members of the Council, including, more particularly, the Soviet delegation, to obtain all necessary information on this matter.*

Mr President (M. Cornut-Gentille, France): *So far, however there is every reason to believe that the foreign intervention was spontaneous and that it occurred before any appeal made by the Hungarian Government. Moreover, that appeal was not made until after the night of October 23/24, when the Soviet troops intervened. There was therefore no justification in the Warsaw Treaty for their intervention, for according to article 4 of that Treaty its members are allied against foreign aggression only, it could be certainly invoked by the Hungarians against the Russians, but not by Hungarians against Hungarians . . .*

United Nations Verbatim Record, Security Council.
New York, October 28 1956

The rebellion is called, in the three-Power letter, a 'situation' and neither the Soviet Union nor its supporting satellite armies or police forces is identified as 'a party to the dispute', which under the Charter, may not vote in any debate about it. The three Western delegates saw no hope that the Russians would accept such a stigma, and it might only have taunted them into writing a violent counter-charge.

They are likely to do so as it is, for last night the Moscow radio, Pravda *and* Isvestia *were mobilized to launch the version that 'imperialist circles in the U.S., U.K. and W. Germany are interfering in the affairs of Socialist countries.*

Alistair Cooke, *Manchester Guardian*, October 28 1956

At various points in the main streets open suitcases had been placed on the ground; they were for donations for aid to the wounded and homeless, and for the families of the freedom fighters who had been killed. They were full of notes, many hundred-forint notes among them. They were unguarded.

Dora Scarlett, *Window onto Hungary*, [n.d.]

The streets looked like a battlefield, and in some places the material damage caused by the fighting was on a scale comparable to that done during the siege of Budapest in 1945. The once splendid Ring Street and the fashionable shopping areas were in ruins, and in many parts of the town torn-up tramway lines, hanging electric cables, burnt-out tanks, overturned motor buses, scattered glass, rubble and cartridge cases bore mute witness to the fierceness of the fighting. For example, on Calvin Square, where heavy fighting had taken place, there were sixteen burnt-out Russian tanks with the crews dead inside them.

International Confederation of Free Trade Unions,
Four Days of Freedom, Brussels, 1957

Radio Free Gyor has just demanded dissolution of the Warsaw Pact and free secret elections.

Radio Kossuth. Budapest, October 28 1956 [15.30]

In the morning a bus trundled through Budapest packed full and with passengers clinging to the outside. The only other traffic on the streets was wagons and cars filled with soldiers and freedom fighters. Many carried the emblem of the Red Cross. The restaurants, theatres and cinemas had been shut. The only people doing a roaring trade were the newsagents. Before the uprising there had been five dull newspapers. Now there were twenty-five.

Beside the Danube, near the Parliament Building, the Duna Hotel was crowded with Western journalists. The hotel's two telephone switchboard operators on the fourth floor were deluged with requests for lines to the outside. There was a twelve-hour delay in getting through. Peter Fryer managed to route his reports via the *Daily Worker's* Moscow correspondent, Sam Russell. The hotel was a hotbed of rumour.

At Party Headquarters the Central Committee of the Communist Party handed its powers to a small team of six: Kadar was its leader; the other members were Antal Apro, Karoly Kiss, Ferenc Munnich, Imre Nagy and

Zoltan Szanto. Nagy was now able to announce further decisions to the people in the hope of gaining their greater confidence: the Uprising had been generated by a general loathing of the crimes of the former régime; the Government must satisfy the people's legitimate demands; there must be an immediate cease-fire; there would be a general amnesty; a new police would be established to replace the AVO, which would be disbanded; the Soviet Star would be replaced with the emblem of Kossuth and March 15, the anniversary of the 1848 Revolution, would once more be a national holiday; the Soviet troops would leave Budapest once the new police force had been set up and there would be Hungarian-Soviet discussion about the withdrawal of Soviet troops stationed elsewhere in Hungary. Nagy was confident his package would appeal to the rebels. He had a majority of support amongst the six-man Praesidium. Only the names of Apro and Kiss showed there were still Stalinist-Rakosi sympathizers still in place. But at least they were in the minority and it looked as though Nagy had the genuine support of the Communist Party.

The free radio stations in the provinces relayed the news that the resolutions of workers, students and intellectuals had been acknowledged and many respected. It seemed to be a substantial step in the right direction towards a new form of socialist democracy.

With pressure from without, in the world's press and at the United Nations in New York, Khrushchev must clearly have understood the time had come to seek a resolution of the Soviet Union's conflict with Hungary. He cannot have been unaware that both Yugoslavia and Poland had communicated their sympathy to Budapest. With the lines open either direct to Nagy or through the Soviet Ambassador, Yuri Andropov, Moscow was able to monitor developments by the minute. No doubt it consented to the offers made by Nagy in his broadcast in the afternoon.

Sunday evening saw crowds gathering in anticipation of a withdrawal and Nagy slept the night at the Headquarters of the Communist Party on an improvised camp-bed. Not everyone had given him their trust. A student, Laszlo Beke (a pseudonym) recalled:

We held a meeting later in the evening, at the Engineering University, and talked over every aspect of Nagy's speech. He probably didn't trust Hungary's youth, and principally the students, because of our part in the revolt: we had been the organizers of demonstrations that launched a full-scale war. He knew we would never support a half-way stab at freedom through a Titoist type of government.

The only thing to do was to strengthen our ranks and keep our arms. We would see what tomorrow would bring.

Soviet tanks and troops crunched out of this war-battered capital today carrying their dead with them. They left a wrecked city where the stench of death already rises from the smoking ruins to mingle with a chill fog from the Danube River. I arrived here today from Warsaw by plane, car and foot, walking the last five miles . . .

No sooner were we on the road north to Budapest than we ran into a massive southbound Soviet convoy headed by two armoured cars. Ten T-54 tanks, their Red stars still visible through the grime of gunpowder, oil and blood, waddled behind, leaving Budapest behind . . . On the back of one tank lay the corpse of a Soviet soldier, his eyes staring vacantly back at the Hungarian capital. Other bodies were in the trucks. The Russian tankmen in their black crash helmets looked tired and grim. They were retreating for the first time since they steam-rollered out of mother Russia into Central Europe during World War II. Whether they are moving on order from Moscow is not known.

A Hungarian peasant spat on one tank as it passed him an arm's length away. The Russian crew did not notice. Hatred literally oozed from the Hungarians who silently lined the roadsides watching the Soviets evacuate Budapest. The Russians were nervous but alert. They manned their 100 millimeter tank cannon which were zeroed at the horizontal for firing straight ahead if necessary. And they held tightly to the handles of machine-guns mounted in the tank cockpits and on truck tops . . .

It is doubtful if the Soviets have ever churned up such hatred, anywhere, anytime.

A. J. Cavendish, United Press. October 29 1956

'From October 29 until November 4, for 150 hours, Hungary lived under the great illusion of the most precarious independence of its history.' This was Miklos Molnar's view of the withdrawal. The Communist Party had lost its influence over a country of 9,863,000 inhabitants. Of these, 1,850,000 lived in the centre of the Revolution, Budapest, and the capital was the administrative, economic and cultural heart of the country. The Party had lost control of it just as it had also ceased to be the key influence in the most concentrated area of Hungary's heavy industry in the southern part of Greater Budapest, Csepel Island. It had effectively lost control of Hungary's second largest town, Miskolc, to the north-east;

Szeged in the south; Debrecen on the eastern edges of the Great Plain near the Rumanian border and Gyor in the west. The country had to achieve, for the sake of survival, at least some form of *modus vivendi* with the Soviet Union. Even though the Soviet Army units were leaving it would not be possible for Hungary to fight successfully the second most powerful military nation in the world.

Thoughts of such compromise were far from the minds of the rebels who now celebrated the Soviet withdrawal as a victory. Even the first falls of fine snow did not deter families who took picnics in the parks from sharing their *barack* and sausages. The children collected up the empty cartridge shells as souvenirs. The drunken happiness of the revellers contrasted starkly with the sight of the dead on the streets. Many of the dead Russians lay where they had fallen, hurriedly covered with lime. People searched for missing relatives amongst the lines of corpses, turning over the flags serving as shrouds to inspect the dead.

Nagy asked Colonel Kopacsi 'to organize the new special police force', to recruit rebels and find a suitable candidate to command the force. The chosen officer was General Bela Kiraly.

The stations and barracks of the AVO were opened up. Secret files, photographs – the paraphernalia of the terror police – were heaped on to fires and burned. The municipal council hurriedly renamed Stalin Road 'Street of Hungarian Youth'; Stalin Bridge, 'Arpad Bridge' and Stalin Square, 'Gyorgy Dozsa Square'.

Nagy hastily appointed Ferenc Donath to take charge of radio and information services; and formed a secretariat of Ferenc Janosi, his son-in-law, and Colonel Kopacsi's brother-in-law, Gyorgy Heltai. Even the President of Parliament, Istvan Dobi, was left in no doubt where the new authority came from. Nagy appointed an old friend, Jozsef Szilagyi, his personal secretary to handle appointments and deal with his telephone calls. He had the complete support of Kadar. Even the Rakosi-Stalinists came with him.

Outside the Parliament Building Nagy was spotted by the crowd. When they recognized him they at once launched a barrage of questions, as Tibor Meray records:

> An attractive, rather distinguished-looking woman, her eyes filled with tears, spoke haltingly:
> 'It is good to see you, Comrade Nagy. Everyone was saying that you were a prisoner.'
> Nagy's smile broadened.
> 'You see how much I am a prisoner!'
> He looked about him. He was surrounded by his friends, the little people of the capital. He spoke as though his personal liberty had not been subjected to the slightest restraint during the days just past.
> A man in working clothes asked what was going to happen.

'Go back to your work, Comrade,' Nagy replied, in a tone of encouragement, 'and have no fear ... Return to your work ... Everything will be arranged in the end.'

'That's really somebody,' the young workman said, as he left. 'That's the man we need!'

Nagy strolled gaily on toward the door of the Parliament Building nearest the bridge. Never before, perhaps, had he been so sure of what he was doing as he was on this morning of the twenty-ninth of October. He had read the demands of the Revolutionary Committee of Hungarian Intellectuals. He had found them excessive and had become angry. Instead of helping the Government, these hot-heads were pressing it at the wrong moment. It was not such improvised demands which were needed at this moment. What was needed was a programme whose points would stand the scrutiny of an objective and scientific analysis. It was his intention to proceed calmly and reasonably, and to get to the bottom of the problems.

In the midst of a revolution, he still saw himself as a man of science.

As a self-defined man of science Nagy now tried to work out the correct ways of preserving Hungarian socialism. He had the apparent advantage of being an independent leader; at least he felt he had won his freedom for the expression of his own political beliefs. A new brand of Hungarian socialism would be for the best for Hungary *and* the Soviet Union.

He could take comfort from Marshal Zhukov, Soviet Minister of Defence, who that evening attended a reception at Turkey's Embassy in Moscow. There Zhukov told a journalist: 'In Hungary, the situation has improved. A Government has been formed in which we have confidence ...'

Zhukov was asked about the withdrawal of Soviet troops. Cagily, he answered his enquirer: 'The sooner the activity of anti-national and anti-democratic elements stops, and if there is no danger, the sooner would the Soviet troops withdraw.'

In the circumstances it was a relatively jovial encounter. If anyone recalled Stalin's observation in the past on such obliging remarks they did not say so: 'It is not for nothing that the proverb says, "An obliging bear is more dangerous than an enemy" ...' The old tyrant would soon be proved correct.

DEAR LISTENERS! We are opening a new chapter in the history of Hungarian Radio. For many years now the radio was nothing else but an instrument for disseminating propaganda and lies ...

All those who have broadcast lies from this station in the past have been evicted and have nothing more to do with the Hungarian radio. From this hour our radio is going to be entitled to carry the names of Kossuth and Petofi. The people speaking into these microphones are for the most part new men. From now on you will hear new voices speaking on old wavelengths. From now on, in the messages sent from this station you will hear the truth, as the old oath goes 'the whole truth, and nothing but the truth!'

Several former leading members of our staff as well as several correspondents of the station have been dismissed

(signed) *THE REVOLUTIONARY COMMITTEE OF THE HUNGARIAN RADIO*

Free Radio Kossuth. Budapest, October 30 1956 [15.06]

'The Russians went away and we came out,' a freedom fighter told John MacCormac, the correspondent of the *New York Times*. 'We never surrendered.' The freedom fighter spoke in German and only told John MacCormac his name once he was certain who MacCormac was. The exchange took place outside Maleter's Kilian Barracks. The freedom fighters, amongst them a ten-year-old boy and a fifteen-year-old girl, carried machine guns slung over their shoulders and hand-grenades stuffed in their belts. Some of their arms had been stolen from the dead Soviet soldiers. They were exhilarated and very tired. Another rebel told MacCormac and other journalists to go. He 'didn't like some of the people around here. We have some scores to settle.' The journalists left.

Elsewhere in the capital AVO men were hunted out and hanged from the trees.

Mikoyan and Suslov returned to Budapest with Moscow's outline of events and a solemn declaration acknowledging the Hungarians' rights to determine their own future. It was carefully worded and sounded convincing. It was enough to persuade Nagy that now he could broadcast to the people their entitlement to a new political system:

The National Government, in full agreement with the Praesidium of the Hungarian Workers' Party, has decided to take a step vital for the future of the whole nation, and of which I want to inform the Hungarian working people ... the cabinet abolishes the one-party system and places the country's Government on the basis of democratic co-operation between coalition parties as they existed in 1945 ... Hungarian brothers, workers and peasants: Rally behind the Government in this fateful hour! Long live free, democratic and independent Hungary!'

Nagy finished broadcasting at just before three that afternoon and was followed on the air by Zoltan Tildy, Minister of State; Ferenc Erdei, First Deputy Minister of the Council of Ministers; Janos Kadar, First Secretary of the Hungarian Communist Party. They were all in accord, with themselves and with the Hungarian people.

News of what were interpreted as Soviet concessions delighted President Eisenhower and the Director of the Central Intelligence Agency, Allen Dulles. China declared itself in favour. News reached Budapest that world opinion supported Hungary in the face of the Soviets. His people, that was how *Kulak* had always thought of his compatriots, had reason to feel pleased with the outcome of the struggle: his people believed they had won a glorious and undeniable victory. There were, however, some exceptions.

The red-whiskered Attila Szigeti telephoned Nagy to say that the free elections must take place within three months. If they did not, Szigeti warned, tens of thousands of demonstrators would march from Gyor on Budapest.

The Americans, clearly, felt they could push the rebels on a bit further. Radio Free Europe encouraged the rebels to fight on. Broadcast after broadcast incited the freedom fighters to further action. The staff of Radio Free Europe's headquarters in Munich was increased and their mission was simply to cause more unrest until the streets once again erupted into violence. It was a cynical and clumsy venture.

Early on that Tuesday morning, Cardinal Jozsef Mindszenty was freed from his prison cell fifty miles from Budapest in Felsopeteny Castle. The Cardinal, leader of several million Catholic Hungarians, had been held prisoner for eight years. He left the castle in an armoured car painted with the colours of Hungary. As soon as he reached Rstag he blessed the crowd and assured them he would 'carry on where I left off eight years ago'. He then returned to his home in Buda.

The violence in Budapest continued. AVO men were shot point blank in Republic Square, an event recorded by the *Life* photographer John Sadovy. A detachment of about fifty AVO men had been hiding inside the Head-

John Sadovy's portrait of Cardinal Jozsef Mindszenty immediately after his release from an AVO gaol as he returned to the episcopal palace in Budapest.

quarters building of the Greater Budapest Communist
Party for almost a week. Not far away was a large food-
store within sight of the local Communist Party offices.
The women who were queuing up outside the food-store
saw a truck deliver a load of fresh meat to the Headquarters. The women immediately protested: the Communist functionaries, so it seemed to them, were brazenly
having meat delivered whilst they were lining up on the
off-chance of getting what they needed. It confirmed
their suspicion that there was indeed still one way of life
for Communist officials and another for the people. The
women told some freedom fighters in the area who
promptly went to the Headquarters and demanded to be
told why the deliveries were being made. Two of them
went into the building and were met by men they at
once recognized as AVO. A furious brief exchange was
followed by the detonation of hand-grenades lobbed
down the stair-well. The freedom fighters made for the
exit; one of them was captured. A familiar pattern of
horrifying violence ensued. Urged on by the women, the
freedom fighters called for the release of their man held
inside the building. They failed to get him out and so
attacked the Headquarters with gun-fire. The AVO
opened up with machine guns.

By chance a meeting was underway inside the Headquarters between a colleague of Nagy who was also a
close friend of Janos Kadar. His name was Imre Mezo,
Secretary of the Greater Budapest Communist Party, a
veteran of the Spanish Civil War who had also fought
with distinction with the French underground in the last
war. Mezo now contacted the Ministry of Defence which
promptly despatched three tanks to quell the disturbance.

Towards the climax of the confrontation, Sadovy
arrived on the scene. His photographs of what then happened are amongst the most extraordinary of any press
photographs and remain probably the most well-known
images of twentieth-century revolution. He describes
what followed:

There was only occasional machine-gun fire from the
top floor, but people were still being careful. At the
front of the building there were thirty to forty dead.
They were lying in a line. As one had been hit the man
behind had taken his place – and died. It was like a
potato field, only there were people instead of potatoes.
Now the AVO men began to come out. The first to
emerge from the building was an officer, alone. It was
the fastest killing I ever saw. He came out laughing
and the next thing I knew he was flat on the ground.
It didn't dawn on me that this man was shot. He just
fell down, I thought. Then the revolutionaries brought
out a good-looking officer. His face was white. He got
five yards, retreated, argued. Then he fell forward. It
was over for him. Six young policemen came out. Their

John Sadovy walked the streets of Budapest alone, frequently sick and in tears recorded the killing. By now the streets were littered with Hungarian and Soviet nameless dead, identities lost beneath the lime.

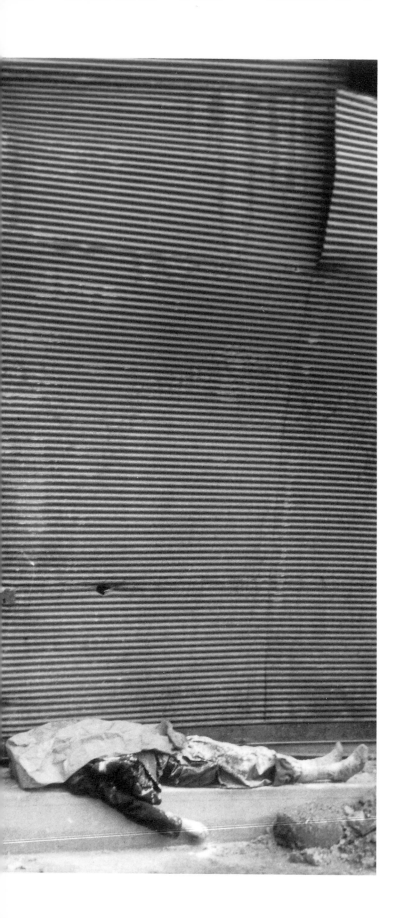

shoulder tabs were torn off. Quick argument. 'We're not so bad as you think we are; give us a chance,' they said. I was three feet from that group. Suddenly one began to slouch forward. They must have been close to his ribs when they fired. They all went down like corn that had been cut. Another came out, running. He saw his friends dead, turned, headed into the crowd. The revolutionaries dragged him out. Then my nerves went. Tears started to come down my cheeks. I had spent three years in the war, but nothing I saw then compared with the horror of this. I could see the impact of bullets on clothes. There was not much noise. They were shooting so close that the man's body acted as a silencer. They brought out a woman and man from the building. Her face was white. She looked left and right at the bodies that were spread all over. Suddenly a man came up and hit her with the butt of a rifle. Another pulled her hair and kicked her. She half fell down. They kicked her again. I thought that was the end of her, but in a few moments she was up, pleading. Some of the revolutionaries decided to put her in a bus which was standing nearby, though there were shouts of 'No prisoners, no prisoners!' There was still shooting inside the building. Occasionally, a small group would come out. One man got as far as the park, which was a long way, but there he was finished. Two more came, one a high-ranking officer. His bleeding body was hung by his feet from a tree and women came to spit at him. Then came a last scuffle at the entrance of the building. They brought out a little boy. They were carrying him on their shoulders. He was about five years old with a sweet expression on his face as he looked left and right. There were shouts: 'Don't kill him, save him!' He was the son of one of the AVO officers from inside the building. To see this little face after what you'd seen a minute ago brought you back to reality. They spared him and the crowd passed him shoulder to shoulder until he was out of harm's way. Going back through the park, I saw women looking for their men among the bodies on the ground. I sat down on a tree-trunk.

The stench of burning flesh filled the square for a corpse of an AVO officer hung upside down from a tree and was burning fiercely. These were revenge killings of atrocious barbarity and Nagy's new police authority was powerless to stop them. They were carried out by freedom fighters as well as by men who had languished in jail for years and were settling scores with fury.

Nagy's colleagues faced the growing tide of street violence with increasing apprehension and with conflicting emotions that generated an atmosphere verging on the chaotic. Viktor Woroszylski, of Warsaw's *Nowa Kultura*, succeeded in gaining an interview with Zoltan Szanto. 'We are living through an immense tragedy,' Szanto told

John Sadovy photographed (*overleaf*) a collaborator who, exceptionally, managed to persuade the crowd to let her live. She was pushed to the ground and left.

Russian dead in the line of Soviet duty.

the Polish journalist. 'Crimes have been committed against the people. The Communists have brought guilt upon themselves. The people are right. We must finally go along with the people. It is already very late as far as the Party is concerned.' Woroszylski described old Szanto's grief as 'terrible'; he had devoted 'all his life to this cause' and was now discovering 'that he was the accomplice of criminals'. Another official urged Woroszylski, 'Believe me, we are no sadists. But we cannot manage to feel sorry for those Hungarians ...' He was, of course, speaking about AVO, men who had subscribed to all the worst beliefs, if that is what they can be called, of policing by terror and liquidation. But they were still Hungarians. It was plain for all to see that Hungarian

In the confusion fleeing AVO-men donned army uniforms for disguise. Sometimes they were betrayed by the boots they had no time to substitute for civilian shoes. Sometimes a Soviet star was dropped on the corpses as a badge, at least, of why a man with no remaining identity had died.

was locked with Hungarian in a terrible fight to the death: evidence all the more poignant when the worst of the revenge killings coincided with the hours in which Nagy, legitimately, might allow himself to feel the disposition of the Soviet Union to Hungary, and his Government, seemed in favour of continuing negotiations to reach a settlement and an end to the tragedy.

Mikoyan and Suslov continued their discussions with Nagy and his Government colleagues. Soviet withdrawal had been agreed, inevitably with the consent of Khrushchev in Moscow. Kadar agreed with Nagy that the troops must be given orders to leave Budapest. But the fighting was still continuing. Not only on the streets. As Noel Barber records: 'Inside the Prime Minister's office in Parliament Building the scene bordered on bedlam. Delegates argued violently. At least two fist fights broke out. Nagy was deeply shocked. After wrestling with his conscience he had just made a broadcast of historic importance, yet instead of being rewarded with praise he could hear in the tumult nothing but more demands, all of which he knew would exhaust Russian patience.'

Nagy was begged to leave the Warsaw Pact. He replied with a furious threat of resignation. 'That would be wonderful!' someone shouted at him. Imre Nagy was on the verge of tears.

In England, another invasion plan, this time of Egypt, was reaching fruition. Sir Anthony Eden summarized it:

> From mid-September until the end of October our forces had been standing ready. During this period, Ministers had frequently examined the state of our precautions in conjunction with the Chiefs of Staff and with the Commander-in-Chief, Middle East Land Forces, General Sir Charles Keightley, who had been appointed Allied Commander-in-Chief for the operation. After much consideration, a plan had been drawn up, designed to secure our objectives with the utmost speed and the least possible loss of military or civilian life.

In Sinai, the Israelis had already launched their four-prong attack during the previous night (October 29). On the evening of Tuesday (October 30) Eisenhower telegrammed Eden who was, according to Eden, 'deeply concerned at the prospect of drastic action'. Eden's almost frantic loathing of Nasser is well-known and is characteristically revealed in the chapters on the Suez adventure in that part of his memoirs called 'The Crunch':

> While the majority of the United Nations was in haste to pillory France and Britain and Israel, not a mouse moved in Arab lands ... Forecasts of universal hate for the Europeans who intervened were not borne out either then or later, because many were hesitant and

John Sadovy recorded (*overleaf*) the mood of melancholy outside the Kilian Barracks where Maleter had led the detachments of the Army sympathetic to the freedom-fighters. Maleter's own tank may be seen backed into the doorway of the two-hundred year old building as a symbol of defiance.

some understood. The West has been as slow to read Nasser's *A Philosophy of Revolution* as it was to read Hitler's *Mein Kampf.'*

Yet, presumably Eden had a vision of adventuring on a scale not entirely dissimilar from Khrushchev's vision of quelling revolution in Hungary. Eden interspersed his Suez account, with an anecdote about Churchill offered, inelegantly, as a moment of light relief:

> One Sunday in October, Sir Winston Churchill invited himself to luncheon at Chequers. On the three-hour journey by car from Chartwell he had dictated a series of questions and suggestions. We had a stimulating discussion which covered every eventuality. As he left, he said: 'I must look up and see exactly where Napoleon landed.'

Nagy stayed put in the Parliament Building late into the Tuesday night. The full horror of what was now about to happen was revealed to him by none other than Colonel Pal Maleter, now Kiraly's Deputy Commander of the Hungarian Armed Forces' Revolutionary Committee. It was Maleter, according to Noel Barber, who reported to Nagy, 'I have to report that Soviet armoured units are invading Hungary in large numbers across the Russian border in the north-east...'

Across Parliament Square some Hungarians were dancing away the night to a tzigane orchestra.

There could be no return to normality as long as disabled Soviet tanks remained in the streets.

Q: *What about the Warsaw Pact now? Are you in it or not?*
Nagy: *At present we are in it.*
Q: *Do you wish to leave the Warsaw Pact, if the Hungarian people desire this?*
Nagy: *Today we have begun negotiations on this matter ...*
Q: *It will now be necessary to reconstruct Hungary economically. Will you apply to the Western Powers for aid in the reconstruction of Hungary?*
Nagy: *It seems to me that we will have to count on all economic forces to help us emerge from this situation...*
Q: *According to the agreement you have concluded, are the Soviet forces now withdrawing to their original bases in Hungary?*
Nagy: *At present the forces in Budapest, it seems, have already withdrawn and have returned to their bases.*
Q: *In Hungary?*
Nagy: *Yes, in Hungary. I do not know exactly where they came from.*
Q: *There are also some Soviet forces which came across the border from other countries. Are they also withdrawing to where they came from?*
Nagy: *I think so, yes. I do not know where they came from, but they will return there.*
Q: *You said just a few moments ago that you were put under pressure to bring in the Soviet troops, that it was not you who invited the Soviet troops to move into Budapest. Who invited them?*
Nagy: *It was not I – that I can say. At that time I was not Prime Minister. I was not a member of the Central Committee of the Party.*
Q: *How then did the impression grow that you invited the troops?*
Nagy: *I do not know. At that time I was not a member of the leadership. It may have been this way: at first it was said it was the Government, and then later on, after two or three days, I was made Premier, and the masses are unable to differentiate. Two days ago or now – it is all the same to them.*
Q: *But did you not approve of the invitation to the Soviet troops afterward?*
Nagy: *No.*
Q.: *Did you say it was necessary for the re-establishment of peace and order, or did you not?*
Nagy: *No, no, no. I did not say such a thing, and I must add that this allegation has caused much damage.*
Q: *What will now be the first measures of the Government?*

Nagy: *We have very grave economic problems. The most important problem is to restore order here, and to re-establish economic life . . .*

Radio Vienna and Rias (Berlin) October 31 1956

We demand that the Russian troops should actually start to leave the country, immediately, because there will be no order, peace or tranquillity on our native soil, sprinkled with precious blood, until they have finally left. We look forward to deeds by the Government and not phrases.

The Workers Council of County Borsod. Free Radio Miskolc [23.35]

BRITISH AND FRENCH FORCES ARE BOMB-ING EGYPT. A member of the Cabinet cursed the news. Nagy was asked once more if, even now, he would make further approaches to the West for help. Nagy replied curtly: 'Certainly not now.' Thus, Chairman Khrushchev received an additional advantage in planning the last acts of the Hungarian tragedy. Great Britain and France had diverted world attention to Suez. The Cabinet adjourned for its morning meeting with a jovial Mikoyan and delighted Suslov. It was a brief meeting. At its end, a reporter from *Igazsag* (*Truth*) watched Mikoyan and Suslov leave and received, by mistake, a hand-shake from Mikoyan:

I found myself in their path, and the Russians – was it by habit or did they take me for a Party official? – shook my hand. Then, rapidly descending the stairs [of the Hungarian Workers' Party on Academy Street] they took their places in a Soviet tank, and the armoured procession started for the airfield.

The moment was, concluded Tibor Meray, 'an episode that was of prime importance to the future of Hungary'.

Mikoyan and Suslov left for Moscow having reaffirmed that the Soviet withdrawal would continue. The Soviet Union, he declared, supported Nagy's Government. Indeed, both *Pravda* and Radio Moscow were announcing with approval that Nagy's Government had the support of the Hungarian people and, presumably by impli-cation, the Government had the support of the Kremlin.

Nagy read the signs of his personal support: the rural areas were quietening down. There were rumours that the West would be disposed to sending help; indeed, medical supplies were getting through from Austria, Britain, France and Switzerland. President Eisenhower offered aid of $10 million. Pal Maleter told journalists that he supported Nagy's Government. The Social Democrats elected the fifty-seven-year-old Anna Kethly their President and Nagy arranged for her attendance at a socialist conference being held in Vienna. He announced

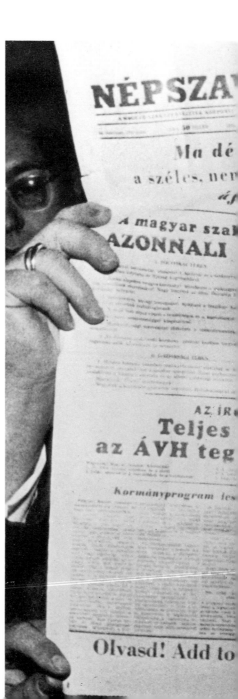

that the charges against Cardinal Mindszenty had no foundation in justice and had been illegal. He spoke to the crowds outside the Parliament building during the afternoon. He was the one, he told them, who had fought for the withdrawal of the Soviet troops. He was calling for the abrogation of the Warsaw Pact. He asked for their patience, 'have confidence in our Government'. He ended with a loud cry: 'Long live the Hungarian Republic, independent, free and democratic! Long live Free Hungary!'

The crowd gave him a massive ovation, unaware that the withdrawal of the Soviet troops was being conducted with extraordinary slowness.

The Revolutionary Committee organized news bulletins broadcast from the town hall and issued their own newspapers.

NOVEMBER 1

Are the Russians returning to Budapest or not? Are the Russians going to stay in Hungary or not? Those are the questions which everybody asks in Budapest.

Lajos Lederer, *Observer* Foreign News Service (London).
November 1 1956

The Russians, we heard, were drawing a ring of tanks around Budapest. They had occupied all the airfields and were permitting no foreign plane to land or take off. Soviet reinforcements were rolling in from the east over the Rumanian border.

Peter Schmid, *Die Weltwoche* (Zurich) and *Commentary*.
(New York) January 1957

Q: *Please tell us something about your part in the battles.*
Pal Maleter: *In the early hours of last Wednesday I received an order from the then Minister of Defence to set out with five tanks against insurgents in the 8th and 9th city districts and to relieve the Kilian barracks. When I arrived at the spot I became convinced that the freedom fighters were not bandits but loyal sons of the Hungarian people. So I informed the Minister that I would go over to the insurgents. Ever since, we have been fighting together and we shall not end the struggle as long as a single armed foreigner is in Hungary.*

Free Radio Kossuth. November 1 1956

Q: *Did Mikoyan and Suslov really come to Budapest during the insurrection?*
Kadar: *Yes – they were in Budapest.*
Q: *And with whom did they confer?*
The minister paused, and then answered: 'I don't know.'

Bruno Tedeschi, *Il Giornale d'Italia* (Rome).
November 2 1956

On the way to the Embassy to telephone to Warsaw, we met Krzyszlof.
  'Have you heard?'
  'What?'
  'Kadar has fled.'

Viktor Woroszylski, *Nowa Kultura* (Warsaw).
December 9 1956

One of the partially destroyed thoroughfares in the area of the Kilian Barracks.

Early in the morning Nagy heard confirmation of what he dreaded: the Soviet troops were not really withdrawing at all; on the contrary, they were coming back.

Budapest's three airports – Ferihegy, Budaors and Tokol – were surrounded by Soviet tanks. Immediately he heard this Nagy telephoned Ambassador Andropov. Andropov told him not to be concerned. The only reason the tanks were there was to make sure Soviet citizens could leave Hungary in complete safety. But Nagy was receiving still more reports of the increasingly threatening stance of Soviet armed forces on the borders. What did it all mean? Nagy at once summoned Ambassador Andropov to his office in the Parliament Building.

Andropov told Nagy blandly that the troop movements were 'completely normal'. He was insistent but the view lacked conviction. Nagy saw the writing on the wall. Could Andropov try and find out of his own accord from Moscow what was happening?

Amongst the onlookers, at the right of the group nearest the tank with its turret blown off is the veteran British correspondent, Trevor Philpot, who generated the special issue of *Picture Post*, CRY HUNGARY, in aid of the refugees and from which the title of the present volume is taken. The author of this volume bought the issue as an eleven-year-old schoolboy along with many thousands of others who reacted with disbelief and outrage at the Hungarian tragedy.

Once again Imre Nagy was trapped. If he said nothing at all to the people still enjoying what they considered to be the fruits of their victory and the intelligence reports were true he would be summarily exposed as, at best, evasive; at worst a liar. He could resign. He had threatened to do so before. But if he did the Soviets would hardly find it difficult to appoint someone as a mouthpiece who would, no doubt, swiftly cast aside what Nagy felt he had achieved. Or, he could be completely honest and painstakingly explain the Soviet treachery to the people and let fate dictate the consequences.

After the first meeting with Andropov that day the Soviet Ambassador telephoned Nagy. Andropov solemnly promised that the Soviet agreement made two days beforehand was unaltered. But when Nagy asked if the Soviet Union was advancing upon Hungary, Andropov said he had no answer. Immediately Nagy called Kadar, Losonczy, Lukacs, Munnich, Szanto, Kiss and Apro, as

chief executives of the Communist Party, to his office and told them he was in no doubt the Soviet Union was acting in direct defiance of the Warsaw Pact. Hungary must issue a renunciation of the Pact and announce its immediate neutrality. There were only two objections: from Szanto and Lukacs.

The meeting of the Hungarian Cabinet that followed took the line that although the Soviets were violating the Warsaw Pact some last effort ought to be made to find a solution. Once again Nagy presented the Soviet Ambassador with the irrefutable evidence of the Soviet advances. He explained to Andropov what his Cabinet advised: leave the Warsaw Pact, declare neutrality, call upon the United Nations in New York to protect Hungary's neutral status. Andropov told Nagy he would see what Moscow felt and let him know in due course.

Determined to retain the unity of his Cabinet Nagy now asked each member in turn for a declaration of their loyalty and support. In Andropov's presence each man did as he was asked. The most passionate declaration was made by Janos Kadar: 'What happens to me is of little importance, but I am ready, as a Hungarian, to fight if necessary. If your tanks enter Budapest, I will go into the streets and fight against you with my bare hands!'

Then Nagy cabled the Secretary-General of the United Nations, Dag Hammarskjöld, asking that Hungary be discussed at the eleventh session of the General Assembly as a matter of priority. He then set off to broadcast to the people, leaving Losonczy to explain developments to the international pressmen in Budapest.

Nagy had, thus, taken the third option: complete honesty. In doing so he, at last, rallied the whole nation behind him.

Just before midnight Nagy went to his villa at Orso Street. On his way home he saw that the windows of the city were filled with candles. In a few minutes it would be All Souls Day, the Day of the Dead. A candle burned in memory of Hungary's martyrs whose ranks had been so tragically increased in the recent days.

Going home to his own bed for the first time in a week Nagy was unaware of two sensational bits of news.

First, his cable to Hammarskjöld had been delayed, lost in the flurry of signals over Suez, or mislaid through administrative oversight. Another message to Hammarskjöld telling the Secretary-General that Janos Szabo, the First Secretary of Hungary's permanent mission, would represent Hungary at the UN Special Session was never received by the delegates. It could hardly have been more urgent; yet the Under-Secretary said, after an interval of one whole day, that he knew nothing about it. By the time Hammarskjöld got round to despatching his acknowledgement of Nagy's desperate cables the lines to Budapest had gone dead.

Second, under cover of night, Kadar had disappeared.

The offices of the newspaper *SZAPAD NEP*.

When Soviet troops began withdrawing from Budapest an unbridled White Terror started in the Hungarian capital. We Soviet tourists recall this time with horror. It is difficult to describe the chaos which reigned in the city where public buildings were destroyed, shops looted, and where crowds of armed bandits, obviously fascists, walked along the streets committing bestial murders in broad daylight.

Some time ago I read how the fascists in Germany burnt progressive literature on bonfires. We saw similar things ...A group of some hooligans looted and set fire to the House of Books. Thousands and thousands of books were smouldering in the muddy street: We were there, witnesses of the barbarity. The works of Chekhov, Shakespeare, Tolstoi, Pushkin, and other famous authors were lying in the mud, black smoke rising. We saw an old man who lifted a few books, then carefully wiped the mud with his sleeve, pressed them to his breast and walked slowly away. Many people did the same.

We shall not forget the Hungarian girl who said that the Hungarians were for socialism and that they were with us.

E. M. Bazarina, Radio Moscow. November 10 1956

Less than twenty-four hours after he had sworn loyalty to Nagy and had broadcast in support of his country's abrogation of the Warsaw Pact, Janos Kadar was at Uzhgorod in the Soviet Union. Why did he go?

His reasons are still shrouded in mystery. Perhaps he resented the influence of the Communist Party being so greatly reduced and it was time to use flight as a gesture of protest. He had no well-established power base to fight the cause of the Hungarian Communist Party whilst a second wave of Soviet violence seemed imminent along with all it entailed. Miklos Molnar considers it unwise to attribute to Kadar either a willingness to stay and fight or to hang on and await some form of Soviet deliverance whose form could hardly be predicted. True, Kadar had played his part in seeing the general drift of the original students' demands fulfilled. But he was completely out of sympathy with the violent mood of the rebels. He perfectly well understood, like his colleagues, that the rebels were Communists like himself. He was also a committed opponent of counter-revolution. He would have viewed with extreme misgivings any action that might lead to intervention from both the Soviet Union and the West,

John Sadovy's portraits of freedom-fighters on this and the following pages show some bemused, some triumphant in the moment of what seemed a people's victory for a future based at last upon justice and decency.

an improbable event but, given the approaches to the United Nations, one that might conceivably occur if things took some very unexpected turn. He had always been a bureaucrat; an official more readily disposed to lead from behind a desk than with grand broadcasts and public speeches. If he saw his move as the best, if not high-risk, step he could take in pursuit of power, then he was subsequently proved entirely right and may be said to be possessed of remarkable political foresight. Perhaps he felt, at forty-four, he had a long political career ahead of him linked to a ship which was sinking fast; that he was the one who could either save it or salvage the wreck. Again, if he felt that, he has been proved correct.

It turned out that Kadar had left along with Ferenc Munnich. They were taken to the Soviet Embassy where they must have conferred with Andropov acting on instructions from Moscow. From the Embassy they were driven across the border to Uzhgorod.

Nagy heard the news of the joint defection in the morning. He decided to make no announcement about it. There were rumours that the arrival of a UN delegation in Budapest was imminent and news of support for him from the Protestant hierarchy. He was certain the whole country supported his plan for the creation of a National Assembly and there was, naturally, complete agreement that there must be no return to any system bearing even the remotest semblance to capitalism. Even if faced with the duplicity of the Soviet Union he had at last achieved the essential pre-requisite for maintaining his own power over the internal affairs of the country: a clear acceptance from many divergent political parties of his ideas and the belief it was now possible to say Hungary was voluntarily united.

In the afternoon Nagy received a message from the Soviet Embassy. He was told the Soviets were prepared to enter into further discussion about the withdrawal of their troops. The United Nations discussed Hungary. Britain and Austria said the matter must be discussed. The French delegate was even stronger in demanding that the Security Council be told whether or not the Soviet troops were re-grouping on Hungary's borders. It was left to the Soviet delegate, Sobolev, to deny the presence of Soviet troops on the borders of Hungary. The Security Council now turned its attentions to the débâcle in Suez.

It was noted in Moscow that Chairman Khrushchev had failed to turn up, as announced, at a reception for the President of Syria. Both Zhukov and Shepilov left early.

In Budapest, a replacement Minister to the American Legation arrived only to find his staff had been already evacuated to Vienna.

The night turned cold. The harsh winds failed to extinguish the candles in the windows although by now they burned low.

Poised in the aftermath of apparent
victory, unaware they had been deserted
by Western powers adventuring in the
Middle East, the freedom fighters
wandered the streets of the city they felt,
at last, was theirs.

NOVEMBER 3

It is said that when a man is fatally sick, he frequently experiences a day of euphoria a little before his death, when the functioning of his organs seems almost normal, giving him the illusion that recovery is possible.

In the history of the Hungarian Revolution, that day was November 3.

Tibor Meray, *Thirteen Days that Shook the Kremlin*, 1958

The sky above Hungary has been bright today: it was a sunny winter day. The atmosphere in the country, particularly in the capital, was somewhat in accordance with the weather. I think that I would not exaggerate by saying that this Saturday has been the first peaceful day since October 23 ...

Djuka Julius, *Politika*, (Belgrade). November 4 1956

The stores also reopened their doors, the food stores among the first. Queues of shoppers lengthened along the streets, waiting to buy bread and potatoes, and the housewives could be sure that they would not have to return home empty-handed. There was no threat of famine in the capital. In the espresso shops, there was already black coffee to be had, and some were even able to serve patisserie. On the street corners, chestnut-sellers offered those paper cones of warm nuts which were so welcome in the crisp chill.

Tibor Meray, *Thirteen Days that Shook the Kremlin*, 1958

The yellow street cars carried many thousands of people to work on the Saturday morning. The general strike was at an end. The railway services were almost back to normal. Everyone's favourite profession seemed to be the bakers who had kept up a continuous supply of bread since the start of the Uprising. The theatres and cinemas prepared to open their doors for the first time in many days. People talked of looking forward to a good night out. The librarians of the Szechenyi Library, correctly believing Budapest had lived through possibly its most important upheaval in modern history, issued a request for people to present revolutionary documents for preservation. They reassured anyone making a donation that such material would be considered as 'confidential ... before the victory of the Revolution is definitive'.

And still the reports of the Soviet troop movements went on,' Dora Scarlett noted. 'We heard that armoured forces held the chief roads at Szolnok, Karcag, Debrecen and Nyiregyhaza, and the bridge-heads of the Tisza and of the Danube at Dunafoldvar. Fresh units moved into place round Budapest. Two armoured trains crossed the frontier at Zahony in the north-east. Two hundred tanks dug in round Szolnok and Abony ... People swung between hope and despair. Hungarians are easily elated; I had generally found them readier to hope than I was, and their hope less tinged with doubt than mine. Now they believed they had won a great victory, and they did not want to believe it would be snatched away from them ... The city was at peace, not a single Soviet soldier was to be seen. There was nothing to do but wait.

At noon the crowds saw the Soviet General Malinin arrive at the Parliament Building, his chest covered with medals, to begin negotiations on Soviet troop withdrawal. His aides brought substantial documents outlining the plans to be agreed. Hungarian transport units would assist the Soviet troops; the Hungarian Army would respect and offer due military courtesies to the Soviet troops. It was to be a formal and orderly withdrawal. There was no question of it being seen as a surrender. Minister of State Erdei prepared a communiqué to be issued after this session had ended. Both sides seemed to

Foodstuff was brought into beleaguered Budapest.

be in agreement. The Hungarian delegation consisted of both Government and military representatives; amongst the latter was Pal Maleter, newly promoted General and Vice-Secretary of Defence. The Soviets promised, according to Erdei's communiqué, 'that no new convoy transporting Soviet troops will cross the border'. The negotiations would, it was agreed amicably, be continued at ten that night at Tokol on Csepel Island, General Headquarters of the Soviet Army.

Elsewhere the demonstrations petered out. The last one of any significance was instigated by supporters of Jozsef Dudas, whose plan to take over the Foreign Ministry and the offices of *Szabad Nep* had failed the day before. Nagy ordered Dudas' arrest. Dudas, who sported black trousers and a Tyrolean hat and wore his coat over his shoulders, was thought to bear a grudge about not being in the Cabinet. Some thought he was a neo-fascist. It was not hard for Nagy to have done with him.

Shortly before ten o'clock, the Hungarian military delegation arrived at Tokol. Ferenc Erdei, General Maleter, General Kovacs and Miklos Szucs joined Generals Cherbanin, Malinin and Stepanov. After an hour's discussion Maleter telephoned General Kiraly with a report that progress was being made. Shortly afterwards the telephone lines to Tokol went dead. One of the soldiers, Sandor Horvath, who had accompanied the Hungarian delegation to Tokol, recalls what happened:

> Towards midnight, about twenty military policemen in green caps burst into the room ... They shouted a password and covered our delegation with their sten-guns ... Through the broken door I was watching our boss ... the others were pale ... only his face didn't change. 'So that was it, was it?' he said to the Russians, standing up calmly. I seized my own sten-gun, thinking that before dying I would still shoot a few rounds at the men in green caps, but it was too late. Two military policemen were already holding me. I tried to get free of them. There was a struggle; I was the stronger. I had again seized the barrel of my sten-gun when the boss called out: 'Stop it! It's useless to resist.' What could I do? His words were my orders and I let my sten-gun be taken away.

General Maleter was personally arrested by the Head of the KGB, General Ivan Serov, a personal friend of Khrushchev's. It is widely believed General Malinin and the Soviet military delegation had no knowledge of the KGB plan to arrest the Hungarians and it is said Malinin was shocked and angered by Serov's action.

Pal Maleter was taken into custody. He was condemned to death and executed on June 16 1958. His first wife and their children eventually found refuge in the United States. His second wife, Judith Gyenes, an agronomist, is believed to be still living in Hungary.

NOVEMBER 4

This is Imre Nagy speaking, the President of the Council of Ministers of the Hungarian People's Republic. Today at daybreak Soviet forces started an attack against our capital, obviously with the intention to overthrow the legal Hungarian democratic Government. Our troops are fighting. The Government is in its place. I notify the people of our country and the entire world of this fact.

> Free Radio Kossuth. Budapest, November 4 1956 [05.19]

Premier Imre Nagy calls Minister of Home Defence, Pal Maleter, the chief of our General Staff, Istvan Kovacs, and the other members of the military delegation who went yesterday at 22.00 hours to the headquarters of the Soviet Supreme Command and who have not returned until now, to come back without further delay in order to take over their respective offices.

> Free Radio Kossuth. Budapest, November 4 1956 [05.56]

The Hungarian Government requests officers and soldiers of the Soviet army not to shoot. Avoid bloodshed! The Russians are our friends and will remain our friends in the future!

> Free Radio Kossuth. Budapest, November 4 1956 [07.14]

This is the Association of Hungarian Writers speaking to all writers, scientists, all writers' associations, academies, and scientific unions of the world. We turn to leaders of intellectual life in all countries. Our time is limited. You all know the facts. There is no need to expand on them. Help Hungary! Help the Hungarians, writers, scientists, workers, peasants and intelligentsia. Help! Help! Help!
(Julius Hay)

> Free Radio Kossuth. Budapest, November 4 1956 [07.56]

SOS! SOS! SOS!

> Free Radio Kossuth. Budapest, November 4 1956 [08.24]

The ultimatum to Nasser had been open knowledge in Moscow since the evening of Wednesday October 31, at the same time as the rumours spread across Budapest about increased Soviet military activity on Hungary's borders. Yet only the day before it had seemed both that the Soviets really were *withdrawing* and that Moscow, in the paper brought to Budapest by Mikoyan and Suslov, was seeking to fulfil the promise in the title of their declaration, 'On Friendship and Co-operation between the Soviet Union and other Socialist States'. Did Moscow ever intend to accept Hungary's move to leave the Warsaw Pact and declare itself a neutral state? Events show it did not. Did Moscow decide to make an apparent withdrawal simply to gain breathing space in which to launch a decisive offensive against Hungary? Did Dag Hammarskjöld decide to concentrate his efforts of mediation in Suez as opposed to Hungary? It is certain that Dag Hammarskjöld took no action in support of Hungary. Did the United States decide to let the Soviet Union pursue its own course in deciding Hungary's fate? Again, that is what happened. Was the Kremlin split between those who genuinely wanted to see Hungary follow the Polish pattern and those who wanted the insurgency crushed militarily once and for all? Either way, it was the latter that happened. We cannot know exactly how events were read in Moscow but the Soviets must

The Freedom Council at Gyor meets to debate the implication of the news just received that the Soviets are returning.

have felt safe from interference from the West. Europe was compromised and divided over Suez; the United States was concentrating on a presidential election; the United Nations was impotent. The Soviet Union advanced 150,000 men and some 2,500 tanks into Hungary as an invasion of force of a most conspicuous and overwhelming strength.

Imre Nagy heard of the invasion just before 4 a.m. after four hours of sleep on his camp-bed in the Parliament Building. Zoltan Tildy was in a nearby room. Of his other friends and colleagues only Ferenc Donath and Jozsef Szilagyi were in the building. Nagy summoned Istvan Bibo, Istvan Dobi, Istvan Kristof and Sandor Ronai. Bela Kovacs tried to join them but was prevented from doing so. Donath prepared a draft of an announcement for Nagy to broadcast from the small radio studio at the other end of the Parliament Building. It was 5.20 a.m. when he told the Hungarian people the Soviet forces had launched an attack on Budapest.

Michel Gordey, of *France-Soir*, felt the ground shake. He looked out from his hotel window and 'saw the horizon light up with sinister flames'.

'I rushed to the telephone switchboard,' called Indro Montanelli of *Corriere della Sera*. 'The whole room was in uproar. I met a poor woman, quite pale, who said to me, "I left the concentration camp last week. I was in for seven years ..."'

Thomas Schreiber, of *Le Monde*, saw a tank column on Bajcsy-Zsilinsky Avenue 'manoeuvring in the direction of Alkotmany Street – probably towards Parliament from where Imre Nagy had sent out his desperate appeal ... The Hungarian News Agency at Feny Street has been partially destroyed by Soviet artillery. All communication with the outside world has been cut off. The bridges connecting Buda and Pest have been occupied by Russians...'

News of the Soviet Union's second invasion brought the freedom fighters back into the streets to prepare their defences. Streets were torn up – high explosive charges were laid beneath up-turned soup plates. This time the Soviets penetrated Hungary with overwhelming force. Resistance was hopeless and the Soviets entered the city and began a relentless blitz shortly after.

At the Duna Hotel, Peter Fryer decided the time had come to take the five-minute walk to the British Legation to seek shelter.

Here some eighty British subjects, Legation staff and British journalists, went down into the cellars hastily converted into a shelter from the Soviet bombardment. Somehow, the indomitable Jimmy Green, who had manned the Legation's radio equipment for two days and nights without sleep, kept the wires open. The staff

canteen did a roaring trade. But its staff found it increasingly hard to keep an eye on who was being fed. The Legation signalled the Foreign Office asking the Government to bear the canteen's financial losses during the crisis. The Foreign Office replied that accountancy rules must be adhered to and that non-staff must make out IOUs. Thus, the books were balanced. When Jimmy Green was on the verge of exhaustion Sir Leslie Fry shared a bottle of champagne with him in his secretary's office. When the Soviet tanks arrived at the entrance to the Legation some British girl secretaries crumpled paper into balls and tossed them at the Soviet armour. Incensed, a Soviet tank commander drove his tank up to the door, lowered his tank gun and poked it straight through the door into the front hall. Lieutenant Colonel Noel Cowley records, in Sir Leslie Fry's elegant memoirs, *As Luck Would Have It*, that, 'had the door been wide enough he would probably have driven his tank inside as well'. Two thousand women demonstrated outside the Legation, singing Hungarian songs and the National Anthem until the Soviets drove their tanks straight into them. Colonel Cowley movingly recalls the emotions of those watching the end of this demonstration – one 'they will never forget'. It was one of the last demonstrations of all.

Peter Fryer left the sanctuary of the Legation and made his way back to his hotel room at the Duna. He found his room strewn with broken glass. He recalls:

> Corpses still lie in the streets – streets that are ploughed up by tanks and strewn with the detritus of a bloody war: rubble, glass and bricks, spent cartridges and shell-cases. Despite their formidable losses in the first phase of the Hungarian revolution, Budapest's citizens put up a desperate, gallant, but doomed resistance to the Soviet onslaught. Budapest's workers, soldiers, students, and even schoolboys, swore to resist to the very end.
>
> In public buildings and private homes, in hotels and ruined shops, the people fought the invaders street by street, step by step, inch by inch. The blazing energy of those eleven days of liberty burned itself out in one last glorious flame. Hungry, sleepless, hopeless, the freedom fighters battled with pitifully feeble equipment against a crushingly superior weight of Soviet arms. From windows and from open streets, they fought with rifles, home-made grenades and Molotov cocktails against T54 tanks. The people ripped up the streets to build barricades, and at night they fought by the light of the fires that swept unchecked through block after block.

At 6 p.m. a radio transmitter in Balatonszabadi broadcast the voice of Janos Kadar:

The Hungarian Revolutionary Worker-Peasant Govern-

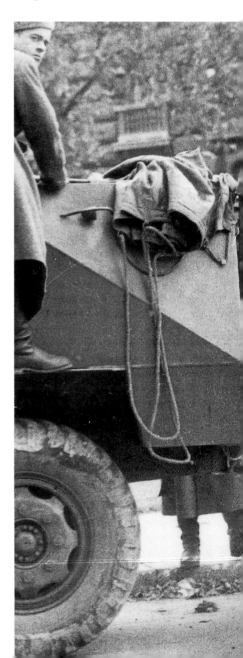

The Jack Esten photograph of the Soviet invaders. The officer with his right hand reaching for his pistol had spotted Esten and Trevor Philpot. Esten, unwell and exhausted had relentlessly photographed the progress of the Uprising accompanied by the fearless Philpot. Immediately the Soviets saw the British pair they screamed at them. The tall man at the back with his mouth open rushed at the diminutive Esten. Esten shielded by Philpot was defiant. The Soviet violently jerked at Esten's camera straps. Philpot, behind Esten, pulled against him until Esten, caught in the middle, began to choke. Finally, Trevor Philpot beat off the Soviet assault and the two journalists escaped with their photographs and their lives.

ment has been formed . . . Our socialist achievements, our people's State, our worker-peasant power, and the very existence of our country has been threatened by the weakness of the Imre Nagy Government and the increased influence of the counter-revolutionary elements who edged their way into the movement. This has prompted us, as Hungarian patriots, to form the Hungarian Revolutionary Worker-Peasant Government.

He then announced that he was Premier. His Deputy Premier and Minister of the Armed Forces and Public Security Force was Ferenc Munnich.

The fourteenth element of his Government's programme, Janos Kadar declared (as the one action it had already taken), was as follows:

The Hungarian Revolutionary Worker-Peasant Government, acting in the interest of our people, working-class and country, requested the Soviet Army Command to help our nation smash the sinister forces of reaction and restore order and calm in the country.

One of Nagy's last visitors in the Parliament Building was Cardinal Mindszenty who had come to seek protection. Nagy advised the Cardinal to seek sanctuary at the United States Mission.

Two hours later, Nagy was told the Soviet tanks were preparing to attack the Parliament Building. Accompanied by Losonczy, Lukacs and Szanto, Nagy left the Parliament Building for the last time by car, to be driven to the Yugoslav Embassy where they asked for asylum.

Others joined them: Donath; Janosi, Nagy's son-in-law; Tanczos; Rajk's widow; Haraszti; some members of their families including children.

The Soviets now launched an air attack on Budapest. The freedom fighters once more took to the streets against the tanks. This time, if snipers took up positions in the buildings, the Soviets simply destroyed the buildings and the snipers with them. Throughout the day the rebel radio stations broadcast their appeals for help to the outside world in vain. Peter Fryer recorded that the Soviet troops began looting. He gained the impression that many of them did not even realize they were in Hungary anyway. 'They thought at first they were in Berlin fighting German fascists.' Not a single freedom fighter was left alive in the Kilian Barracks.

Thousands of Hungarians fled their homes to the Austrian border. Some were solitary children. One group had labels strung about their necks: 'Look after our children; we stay to fight to the last . . .'

At the border, a student recalled:

Abruptly we realized we were only yards away from Austria. Eva [his wife] gave a little cry, reached down where we had stopped, and scooped up a handful of soil. She crushed it in the palm of her hand, and we ran towards the light. We saw an elderly, short, slightly bald man with a sparkling lantern and a smile that shone out just as brightly.

Eva looked at the earth she still clutched in her hand. 'Give me your handkerchief, Laszlo!' she said. 'We're going to take this with us!' She tied a knot in the handkerchief around the precious bit of Hungarian soil, then tied it to her belt.

'Follow me,' the man with the lantern said.

It was as easy as that.

'Follow me' - and we were free.

Three days later Janos Kadar arrived back in Budapest where he has remained ever since.

Imre Nagy, born in Kaposvar in 1896, was executed some time before June 16 1958.

Geza Losonczy, born near Debrecen in 1917, died in prison in unknown circumstances, some time before June 1958.

Pal Maleter, born in Kosice, Czechoslovakia in 1920, was condemned to death and executed with Imre Nagy.

Miklos Gimes, born in Budapest in 1917, was condemned to death and executed with Imre Nagy.

Jozsef Szilagyi, born in Debrecen, date unknown, was condemned to death and executed with Imre Nagy.

Sandor Kopacsi, born in northern Hungary in 1920, was sentenced to life imprisonment in June 1958.

Ferenc Janosi, born in Vajdacska, date unknown, was sentenced to eight years' imprisonment on June 17 1958.

Zoltan Tildy, born in 1889, was sentenced to six years' imprisonment on June 16 1958 and was released in April 1959.

Miklos Vasarhelyi, born in Rijeka, Yugoslavia in 1919, was sentenced to five years' imprisonment on June 17 1958.

The wounded and the dead are not forgotten.

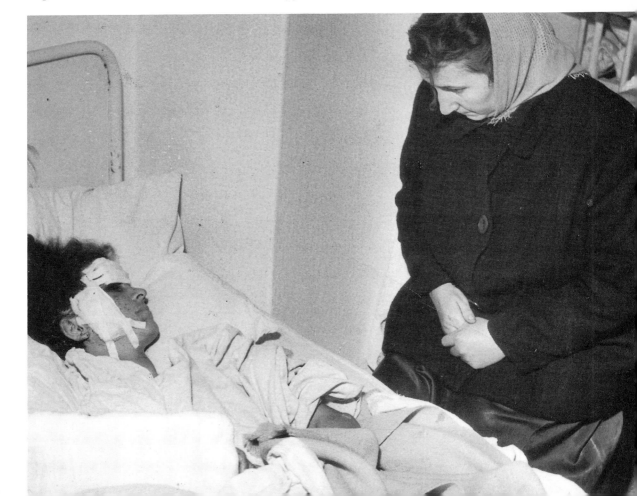

The dead remembered on All Souls' night in 1956 (*right*) when Budapest was illuminated by candles in the streets and in every window.

Appeals for help from abroad were
unanswered. Refugees from Hungary
poured across the frozen borders in their
thousands. Their numbers have never been
exactly calculated. They left on foot, by
bicycle, by horse and cart. Many of the
children came alone.

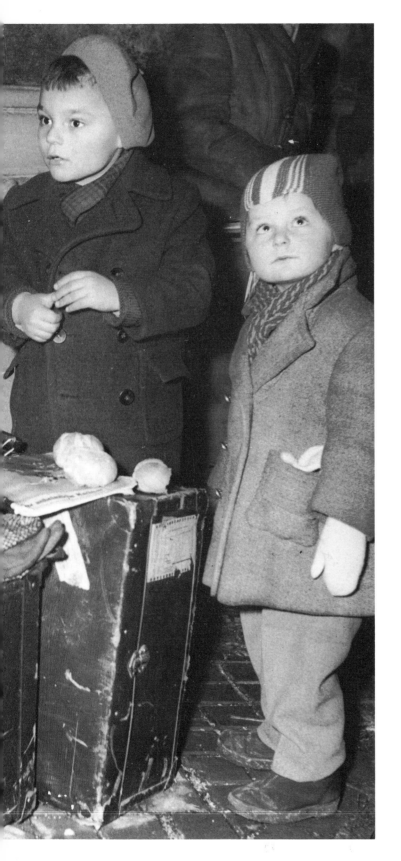

Three years later (*left*) Chairman
Khrushchev attended the Hungarian
Communist Party Congress of 1959. He
was greeted by Janos Kadar. For others
(*right*) the past could not be so easily
forgiven and forgotten.

CHRONOLOGY

October 23

Demonstrations and marches in Budapest. Demands for Imre Nagy to assume leadership and widespread reform of government. Nagy addresses crowds in Parliament Square. Erno Gero broadcasts. First violence erupts at the Radio Station. Statue of Stalin is felled and broken up. Occupying Soviet military moves to quell people's spontaneous revolt.

October 24

Uprising grows beyond Budapest. Nagy, re-appointed to Central Committee of the Hungarian Communist Party, replaces Andras Hegedus as Prime Minister. Direct conflict between people, the Soviet military and AVO. Nagy's appeals for an end to the uprising go unheeded.

October 25

Erno Gero is replaced by Janos Kadar as First Secretary of the Hungarian Communist Party. Street violence continues in site of both Nagy's and Kadar's separate promises of a negotiated withdrawal of Soviet occupying forces.

October 26

Uprising spreads nationwide. Communist Party promises of reforms fail to prevent growing violence.

October 27

Nagy's new Cabinet comprises leaders from other parties but remains, of course, Communist.

October 28

Amnesty offered to all freedom fighters. Nagy's Government committed to abolition of AVO. Nagy heads a committee within the Politburo to deal with growing crisis comprising Antal Apro, Janos Kadar, Karoly Kiss, Ferenc Munnich and Zoltan Szanto. Demands for reform intensify and include more than Government appears prepared to offer.

October 29

Intense fighting involving Hungarian troops sympathetic to freedom fighters. (Israeli invasion of Sinai Peninsula.) Slow start to Soviet troop withdrawal.

October 30

Janos Kadar gives support to Nagy's coalition. Cardinal Mindszenty freed after more than seven years in jail. Spread of non-official radio broadcasts. Colonel Pal

Maleter declares support for freedom fighters. (UK and France issue ultimatum to Egypt and Israel demanding cease-fire and troop withdrawal ten miles from Suez. Egypt refuses.)

October 31
Maleter promoted General and appointed Deputy to Minister of Defence. Mass release of political prisoners. Widespread revenge against AVO and public killings. (Anglo-French forces launch bomb attacks against Egyptian airfields. Public protest in UK against Suez adventure. US airlifts aid to Israel.)

November 1
Imre Nagy announces Hungary's neutrality and withdrawal from Warsaw Pact. Soviet forces re-deploy. (UK forces take Gaza.)

November 2
Nagy signals UN and issues appeals to world powers.

November 3
Soviet troops close in on Budapest. (UK and France accept cease-fire.) Kadar and Munnich disappear. Maleter arrested.

November 4
(UN agrees to send troops to Middle East.) Soviet forces launch massive dawn attacks on Budapest. Kadar and Munnich broadcast from across border in sympathy with Soviet action. (UN agrees to debate crisis in Hungary.) Freedom fighters appeal to world. Soviets crush resistance with great savagery.

November 5
(British parachute troops at Port Said. Soviet rocket threat to UK and France.) Continued appeals to West for help.

November 6
(President Dwight D. Eisenhower re-elected in US election.) Further appeals to West but free radio stations are over-run.

November 7
(Anglo-French cease-fire over Suez.)

November 8
Soviet withdrawal from Hungary demanded by UN General Assembly.

INDEX

ACKNOWLEDGEMENTS

The photographs are reproduced by kind permission of the following:

BBC Hulton Picture Library: 1, 48(l), 57(a), 62–3, 64–5, 81, 90, 91, 129(r), 132–3, 164–5, 166–7.

Camera Press: 26, 42–3, 128–9, 142, 171.

John Hillelson: © *David Hurn* 61, 146–7, 148–9; © *Erich Lessing* 3, 14, 48–9, 49(r), 50–1, 52, 60, 66–7, 120, 144, 150–1, 156–7.

The Photo Source: 17, 27, 32, 38, 65(r), 68, 69, 82, 99, 131, 159.

Popperfoto: endpapers, 2, 6–7, 18–19, 33(r), 36, 46, 56(l), 98, 101, 102–3(a), 122–3, 145, 153, 155, 169, 173(b), 174, 175.

Rex Features: 29, 93, 162–3, 172, 173(a).

John Sadovy: 10, 11, 43(r), 70, 71, 74–5, 78, 79, 83, 84–7, 88, 92, 95, 112, 114(l), 115, 116, 118(l), 118–19, 119(r), 124(l), 124–5, 126, 137, 138, 139, 140, 143, 170, 176–7.

Frank Spooner/Gamma: 56–7, 94, 106–7, 135.

Syndication International: 28, 39, 54, 62(l), 75(r), 102–3(b), 121, 176(l).

Topham: 20–1, 47, 160(l), 160–1, 178, 179.

Picture research by Tomás Graves.